The Parthenon Frieze

The Parthenon Frieze

Ian Jenkins

THE BRITISH MUSEUM PRESS

In memory of Ivor C. Jenkins,
my father

Frontispiece Poseidon, Apollo and Artemis
(cast from east frieze VI, in Athens).
Page 6 Youths restraining one of the
sacrificial victims (south frieze XLIV,
British Museum).

© 1994 The Trustees of The British Museum
Published by The British Museum Press
A division of The British Museum Company Ltd
46 Bloomsbury Street, London WC1B 3QQ

First published in paperback 2002

British Library Cataloguing in Publication Data
A catalogue record for this book is available
from the British Library

ISBN 0–7141–2237 8

Designed by James Shurmer
Cover designed by LewisHallam

Printed in Great Britain by
Butler & Tanner Ltd, Frome and London

Contents

Preface

Who are these coming to the sacrifice?
To what green altar, O mysterious priest,
Leadest thou that heifer lowing at the skies,
And all her silken flanks with garlands drest?
What little town by river or sea shore,
Or mountain-built with peaceful citadel,
Is emptied of this folk, this pious morn?
And, little town, thy streets for evermore
Will silent be; and not a soul to tell
Why thou art desolate, can e'er return.

The calm and understated beauty of the Parthenon frieze impresses us now, as it did the poet John Keats, who saw it when it was first displayed in London nearly 200 years ago. His *Ode on a Grecian Urn*, with its opening lines, 'Thou still unravished bride of quietness, / Thou foster-child of silence and slow time', was in part inspired by a viewing of the frieze and brilliantly captures its mood of perfect tranquillity, calling to mind Plutarch's testimony to the particular qualities of Athenian art of the age of Pericles. Plutarch was writing in the second century AD, some five or six hundred years after the Parthenon was built, and for him all the works of Pericles' day had about them a bloom of perpetual youth. And yet, he acknowledges, such was their grandeur when first created that they seemed already antique (*archaios*). It was this air of freshness, on the one hand, and venerability, on the other, that gave the art and architecture of Periclean Athens its unmistakable character, all the more remarkable for having been created so quickly. These were, in Plutarch's words, 'works that had come into being in a short time in order to last for a long time'.

This book has been some twenty years in the making, that is to say twenty years of thinking, talking about and ultimately writing about the Parthenon frieze. It would perhaps have been as well to wait another twenty years, but art is long, while life, if not necessarily short, does not always offer the same opportunity twice. The opportunity for writing this book came at the suggestion of my editor Teresa Francis, who saw that the subject has for some years now needed an up-to-date summary in English for students and the general reader, the account by Martin Robertson and Alison Frantz (1975) being long out of print.

A book of this kind owes a great deal to the work of others, some of which is acknowledged in the bibliography. In this, however, I have been deliberately sparing so as not to encumber the narrative with the weight of previous scholarship, which is both vast and complex. The chief reason for the scale of this literature is the preoccupation of scholars with the meaning of the frieze: although the broad theme of the subject matter can be readily understood as a festival procession, there is much uncertainty as to its precise meaning, if any. The first part of this book discusses the problem in detail and is frequently critical of the excessive theorising that goes on in the search for a definitive answer. Here it has been necessary to heed the warning of John Boardman, who has remarked upon how 'scholars readily dismiss the theories of others on this matter as over-complicated or obscure, in all ways inferior to their own obscure and overcomplicated suggestions'. The only way out of this maze is a return to the first principles of *looking*, and if I have exercised my own capacity to speculate on the meaning of the frieze, it is not with the intention of finding a once-and-for-all solution, but with a view to establishing a common ground founded upon close observation of the sculpture itself.

The second part of the book aims to facilitate this looking by attempting a complete restoration of the frieze accompanied by a detailed commentary. Reconstructing the frieze *in toto* is a large undertaking and I confess to not having realised, before compiling this book, the extent to which major questions had hitherto been left unresolved. Some detailed notes on the problems can be found on pages 49–51, while here I must acknowledge the help I have received from Madeleine Gisler-Huwiler and Professor Ernst Berger, whose forthcoming publication will present the results of their own extensive research into the original arrangement.

This is based upon the near-miraculous reconstruction in the Skulp-turhalle in Basel, of the Parthenon sculptures in plaster cast. This enterprise, initiated by Berger, represents a major achievement in the study of the Parthenon sculptures. I have also had valuable assistance from Professor Evelyn Harrison and Dr Manolis Korres, both of whom in different ways have greatly enhanced our understanding of the Parthenon and its sculptures. I must acknowledge also my debt to Dr Anastasia Dinsmoor for assisting my study of the papers of W. B. Dinsmoor in the library of the American School of Classical Studies in Athens, and to the Caryatids (Friends of the Department of Greek and Roman Antiquities at the British Museum) and Professor John Camp for facilitating my research during frequent visits to Athens. I owe special thanks to Sue Bird, whose painstaking drawings are a major part of this book, to James Shurmer for making sense of one of the most complicated design problems he has ever faced, and to Julie Young for seeing it through press. Arthur Searle helped me to formulate a musical analogy for the frieze. Lucilla Burn, Brian Cook, Lesley Fitton, Teresa Francis, Brunilde Sismondo Ridgway, Dyfri Williams and Susan Woodford all read the text and suggested many corrections and improvements. Other thanks go to Judith Binder, Peter Calligas, Frances Dunkels, John Leopold, Alexander Mantis, Olga Palagia, Ismene Triandi and Christina Vlassopoulou. Last, but not least, I wish to acknowledge my debt to the hundreds, if not thousands, of Museum visitors and students whom I have been privileged to guide around the sculptures and from whom I have learned a great deal. This book is intended for them.

Colour Plate II
Lawrence Alma-Tadema:
*Phidias and the Frieze
of the Parthenon,*
1868 (detail).
Birmingham Museums and
Art Gallery.

Colour Plate III
The Panathenaic Way in the
Athenian *agora*, with the
Acropolis in the distance.

Colour Plate IV The west frieze seen through the columns of the Parthenon. (The sculptures have now been removed from the building.)

1 The Parthenon and Athens

The Parthenon and its sculptures

Around 450 BC Athens' premier statesman, Pericles, initiated a programme of works designed to embellish his city in a manner befitting her supreme status among the other Greek states. The Parthenon, begun in 447 and completed around 432 BC, was built on the Acropolis, a great mass of rock rising sharply out of the plain around Athens, and was the crowning achievement of this building programme. The temple, including its roof tiles, was made out of fine white Pentelic marble quarried some ten miles from the city and hauled up to the Acropolis by ox-cart. It was unusual both in its great size and in the lavishness of its ornament, of which the frieze was a part.

The Parthenon frieze is one of three major elements forming the sculpted ornament of the temple, the other two being the *metopes* and the pediments. In Greek the word *metope* means 'between the eyes', and the name is thought to refer to the manner in which each panel alternated with an architectural element decorated by three vertical mouldings and hence called a *triglyph*. The metopes and triglyphs were placed at the same height as the frieze, but in a more conspicuous position above the outer architrave supported by the columns of the peristyle. The Parthenon frieze is, strictly speaking, therefore, one of two friezes. The temple was constructed in the Doric order of Greek architecture, and the metopes were part of the so-called 'Doric frieze' running around the outside. Although unusually rich in the number of metopes that were sculpted, this frieze took the standard form for temples designed in that order.

The metopes numbered ninety-two and represented various mythical battles: on the west side a contest between Greeks and Amazons; on the north, a battle between Greeks and Trojans, as well as other scenes from the legendary sack of Troy; on the south a battle between Greeks and the race of Centaurs, part man and part horse, and on the east a struggle between the Olympian gods and their enemies the giants. Such episodes from Greek mythology were the stock-in-trade of Greek temple sculpture,

1 Cut-away diagram of the east side of the Parthenon, showing the position of the architectural sculptures.

9

but in the context of the Parthenon, as we shall see, they have particular relevance.

The inner frieze, which is the subject of this book, does not take the canonical Doric form, but is borrowed from the Ionic order and consists of an uninterrupted band. It is a mark of the extraordinary lavishness of the building that the architects chose to have this frieze, measuring about 3 feet 3 inches (99 cm) high and some 524 feet (160 m) long, carved with continuous figured sculpture. Comparison may be made with the Hephaesteum, another temple erected by Pericles' administration. It stands very well preserved to this day on a low hill overlooking the site of the ancient market-place of Athens. Although considerably smaller, it has many features in common with the Parthenon. Mitigating Doric severity with Ionic extravagance, it too combines a Doric façade with an inner Ionic frieze, but here carved with figured sculpture only over the two porches.

The other group of carvings ornamenting the exterior of the temple is the pedimental sculpture. This decorated the triangular gable ends on the short sides of the building. While the frieze was cut in low relief and the metopes in very high relief, the pediments were filled with sculpture in the round standing on a narrow shelf forming the base of the triangle. The west pediment is much battered and it would be hard to guess at its subject, were it not for the testimony of Pausanias, who records that it showed the struggle between Athena and Poseidon for the land of Attica. The east pediment has also suffered much, the central figures being almost entirely lost. Again we rely upon Pausanias for our understanding of the subject, the birth of Athena from the head of her father Zeus.

Parthenos and Parthenon

Although today the architectural sculptures of the Parthenon are admired as evidence of the skill of ancient sculptors, in antiquity they were secondary to the colossal image of Athena which stood 40 feet (12 m) high inside the temple. This was designed by Phidias and was veneered with various costly materials, principally gold and ivory. The statue disappeared in antiquity, but a general impression of it can be gained from descriptions by Roman writers and from a number of representations, the most important being smaller-scale copies in marble. The goddess

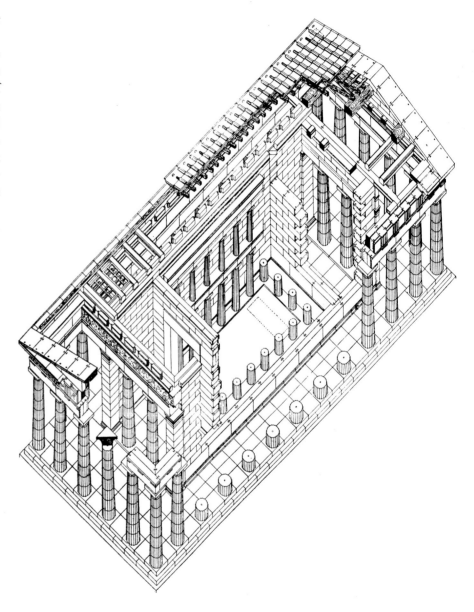

2 Three-dimensional diagram of the Hephaesteum, showing the sculptured Ionic frieze over the porch only.

3 The west pediment of the Parthenon before the explosion of 1687. In the centre are figures of Athena and Poseidon. Athena's chariot is clearly shown on the left side of the pediment, while Poseidon's was on the right. Drawings attributed to Jacques Carrey, 1674.

stood with her hand resting on a shield, within which coiled the sacred snake of the Acropolis. Her right hand supported a figure of Nike, the female personification of victory. Athena's spear was shown leaning against her left shoulder, and on her head she wore an elaborate helmet surmounted by a sphinx flanked by representations of the winged horse Pegasus. The high podium of the statue was ornamented with a frieze representing the gods gathered to witness the birth of Pandora, the first mortal woman. Other subjects adorned parts of the statue itself: on the outside of the shield a battle between Greeks and Amazons was shown in relief; on the inside, painted or engraved, was a contest of gods and giants; and the soles of her sandals carried a battle of Greeks and centaurs. These subjects seem to have been chosen deliberately to echo those of the metopes on the exterior of the temple.

The statue, surrounded on three sides by an interior colonnade, stood at the end of a long room facing the doorway at the east end of the temple. This room was approximately 100 Attic feet long (one Attic foot measured a little more than one of our own) and occupied the greater part of the *cella*, that is to say the space enclosed by the ashlar masonry walls of the building. Separated from the principal room by an interior cross-wall was another smaller chamber with its own entrance from the west, which served as a treasury. The statue is frequently referred to by modern scholars as a cult statue, as if it had been made for an established cult of Athena 'the virgin'. So far as we can tell, however, there was no cult of Athena Parthenos at the time the temple was built. There is some evidence that a cult developed later, but in Pericles' day it seems no prayers were uttered, no dedications made and no sacrifices offered up in the name of Athena 'the virgin'. The principal cult of Athena on the Acropolis was that of Athena Polias, a title formed from the Greek word *polis*, meaning 'city'. Her statue was a primitive idol made from olive wood, so old that its presence on the Acropolis was explained by the claim that it had fallen from the sky in remote antiquity.

How, therefore, is the statue of Athena Parthenos to be explained and, indeed, the temple itself? Rather than resort to the invention of a cult for which there is no evidence, it is safer to assume that the Parthenon and its statue were a grandiose votive designed to commemorate the greatness of Athena, her city, its history and people. As such, both statue and temple were a replacement for an unfinished temple which preceded the building of the Parthenon on the south side of the Acropolis. The remains of this temple, destroyed by the Persians, were partly reused in the building of the later Parthenon. The earlier temple was probably begun shortly after 490 BC in order to commemorate the recent victory of Athens and her ally Plataea over the Persians at the Battle of Marathon.

The Persian wars

If the Parthenon is indeed a replacement for the earlier temple it is reasonable to ask why the Athenians waited for two generations, until around 449 BC, before they decreed its construction. The answer must lie in the oath which, according to an ancient tradition, was sworn by all the Greek allies pledging not to renew their ruined temples until the Persian menace had been removed from Greece, once and for all. There is some uncertainty about how Athens was released from the terms of this pledge, but the likeliest explanation is that she arranged a truce with her Persian enemy, the so-called Peace of Callias. The Peace came after a period of hostilities that had seen great changes in Athenian fortunes. In 492 BC the Persian king Darius had sent his general Mardonius across the Hellespont to take revenge on the Greeks of the mainland for their part in aiding the revolt of the Greek cities of Asia Minor. The latter lived under Persian rule and in 499 BC had staged a rebellion, which proved disastrous. Darius' punitive expedition under Mardonius was unsuccessful and Mardonius himself was injured. The king did not forget his revenge, however, particularly on the Athenians for their part in the rebellion: he even kept a servant whose special duty was periodically to repeat the words, 'Remember the Athenians'. In 491 BC Darius sent envoys to the free Greek states demanding earth and water as symbols of their submission

4 Model of the gold and ivory statue of Athena Parthenos by Phidias. Toronto, Royal Ontario Museum.

Colour Plate I The Parthenon seen from the west.

to the Persian yoke. At Athens these messengers were hurled into a pit, while in Sparta they were pushed down a well and there told to satisfy their thirst.

When eventually the invasion came it was aimed directly at the Athenians, who in one of the most gallant defences in all military history, and with only the help of their neighbour Plataea, routed the vastly superior numbers of the Persian army at the Battle of Marathon. It was therefore in search of a double revenge that in 480 BC Darius' successor, Xerxes, crossed the Hellespont on his way to subdue Greece. Xerxes was the very essence of an oriental despot and is said to have lashed the Hellespont, the notoriously turbulent stretch of sea between the land masses of Europe and Asia, for daring to impede the passage of his army across its stormy waters. The preparations for Xerxes' invasion had taken five years to complete, and when at last the great army was gathered it was, according to the Greek historian Herodotus, the greatest mustering of forces in recorded history. Herodotus recounts the events of the invasion as a vast moral tale of the Great King's perverted attempt to distort the natural east-west balance of the world. Xerxes' excess of ambition was wanton pride, of a kind which might be effective in the short term but was liable ultimately to bring about the wrath of the gods. 'There was not', says Herodotus, 'a nation in Asia that he did not take with him against Greece and, excepting the great rivers, there was not a stream his army drank from that was not drunk dry.'

Athens, meanwhile, under the leadership of Themistocles, had used the proceeds of a lucky strike in the silver mines at Laurium to build up her fleet. In compliance with the Delphic oracle's pronouncement that she should trust in her wooden walls, most of the fighting men took to their ships, and the city was evacuated in advance of the Persian invasion. A few stayed behind, arguing that the oracle meant not the timber hulks of ships but the wooden pallisades of the Acropolis. The valour of Leonidas and his small force of Spartans at the Thermopylae pass failed to arrest the Persian onslaught, and the enemy was soon in the city, sacking and burning the sacred citadel. Themistocles' strategy paid off, however, and on 20 September 480 BC, while Xerxes and his court looked on from the heights above the Bay of Salamis, the allied fleet caught and destroyed the Persian ships in the straits between that island and the Greek mainland.

Xerxes fled dismayed back across the Hellespont, leaving Mardonius in charge of the Persian land army. The following year this was destroyed, and Mardonius killed, at the Battle of Plataea. The Greek allies took the war across the Aegean and into Persian waters. When they arrived at the Hellespont they laid siege to the town of Sestos and eventually took it. Among the spoils the Athenians took home to their triumphant but war-ravaged city were the cables of the bridges Xerxes had thrown across the strait, which were subsequently dedicated at Delphi. For centuries afterwards visitors to the sanctuary were shown these relics of Athens' former glory, and the dedicatory inscription can still be read there today.

The free Greek cities maintained a state of readiness to defend themselves against renewed Persian attacks, and a confederacy was created to formalise the alliance with a base on the sacred island of Delos. First Sparta held the leadership of the alliance, but such a long-term commitment abroad of her military resources ran contrary to Spartan custom, and she soon allowed the captaincy to pass to Athens. Under Athenian control the confederacy, begun as a union of equal partners, gradually lost its high-minded independence. Athens' ambitions to become the premier Greek state squeezed her allies, until they were reduced to the status of satellites in what was, in all but name, an Athenian empire. The original arrangement had required member states to contribute ships and men to the common cause. As Athens' own navy came to rule the waves, however, the other states were pressed increasingly to contribute money instead of ships. When in 454 BC the communal treasury was removed from Delos to Athens, no one was left in any doubt as to the true nature of her intentions. Henceforth she would exact protection money from her subjects, who were not allowed freedom of choice as to whether or not they were to be members of the union.

Pericles' building programme

By these means Athens assembled the funds necessary to finance the ambitious building programme masterminded shortly after the middle of the century by Pericles, her leading statesman. Pericles used his unique powers of oratory to sway the Athenian democratic assembly, and they voted him into power year after year through the 440s and 430s BC. A circle of artists, poets and philosophers gathered around him, including the sculptor Phidias, who became artistic director of the building programme. This centred on the Acropolis, but also adorned the lower town and Athenian countryside with splendid new temples dedicated to the gods on whose continued beneficence Athens' greatness depended.

The temple dedicated to Hephaestus overlooking the ancient market-place has already been mentioned and has features in common with two other temples outside Athens. These are the Temple of Nemesis at Rhamnous to the north-east of Athens and the Temple of Poseidon, dramatically sited on a sheer-cliffed promontory at Sunium to the south. Like the Parthenon, the Sunium temple stands on the foundation of an earlier building still unfinished at the time of the Persian invasion. The fifth major temple put up by Pericles' administration was dedicated to Ares, god of war, and again resembles the Hephaesteum. This building has a peculiar history, since its remains now stand in the centre of the Athenian market-place. The surviving blocks bear masons' marks of the Roman period because the Romans dismantled it and rebuilt it there. No one knows for sure where it was originally sited, but it was perhaps at Acharnai, several miles to the north of Athens, where a shrine to Ares is known to have existed.

The Periclean building programme was conceived partly as a celebration of the city's current prestige and partly in commemoration of Athens' valour during the Persian wars. The Temple of Nemesis, the personification of divine vengeance over excess, was erected a short distance away from the plain of Marathon, where the Athenians who died in the battle were interred in a mound that became a place of pilgrimage for generations. The Temple of Poseidon at Sunium was dedicated to the god of the sea, in whose waters Athens and her allies had gambled against and vanquished the Persian fleet. The Temple of Ares, who had granted victory, needs little explanation. The Temple of Hephaestus, god of smiths, was perhaps shared by Athena who, apart from being patron goddess of the city, was also the protector of craftsmen. The divine intelligence and skills of these two had been bestowed on the city's craftsmen, who were second to none in Pericles' day and for whom he provided work and prosperity. Plutarch, in his *Life of Pericles*, describes the renaissance of the city's artistic community as the various crafts were called upon, including those of the carpenter, moulder, bronze-smith, stone-cutter, dyer, worker in

gold and ivory, painter, embroiderer and embosser. Then there were the support services such as the providers of raw materials, shippers by sea and wagon-drivers by land. By this means everybody came to share in the city's prosperity.

Mention has yet to be made of the little Temple of Athena Nike, goddess of victory, which was built on a rocky spur flanking the court in front of the Propylaea gateway, and of the temple known as the Erechtheum, constructed to an unusual and complex design on the north side of the Acropolis opposite the Parthenon to the south. These temples were not completed until after Pericles' death, but are nonetheless thought to have been conceived as part of his original programme.

It may be wondered what the Athenians themselves made of this rapid and costly resurrection of their temples. Plutarch recounts a clash between Pericles and his political rival Thucydides (not the more famous historian of that name, but another usually distinguished by the epithet 'son of Melesias'). Plutarch's text reads as follows:

Thucydides and his party kept denouncing Pericles for playing fast and loose with the public moneys and annihilating the revenues. Pericles therefore asked the people in assembly whether they thought he had expended too much, and on their declaring that it was altogether too much, 'Well then,' said he, 'let it not have been spent on your account, but mine, and I will make the inscriptions of dedication in my own name.' When Pericles had said this, whether it was that they admired his magnanimity or vied with his ambition to get the glory of his works, they cried out with a loud voice and bade him take freely from the public funds for his outlays, and to spare nought whatsoever. And finally he ventured to undergo with Thucydides the contest of ostracism, wherein he secured his rival's banishment, and the dissolution of the faction which had been arrayed against him.

Since Plutarch was writing more than 500 years after the event, his account is not to be taken literally. He may, however, have been drawing on a contemporary source and, in any case, his version presents the sort of argument that must have gone on in the Athenian democratic assembly, where freedom of speech allowed opinions to be voiced. Pericles was famous for his powers of oratory. None of his speeches survive, but their spirit is captured in the words the historian Thucydides puts into the statesman's mouth in his great narrative of the Peloponnesian War (431–404 BC). In the years leading up to the war, Athens' imperialist ambitions had come increasingly to be resented by her rival Sparta. Eventually, mutual hatred spilled over into outright hostility. The ensuing struggle takes its name from the Peloponnese, the region of Greece in which Sparta was located. It lasted over twenty years and eventually brought Athens to her knees. Thucydides chose the events of the year 431 BC, when Athens was at the height of her power and fame, as the occasion for Pericles' great set-piece speech. It was the end of the first year's campaigning, when there was high hope of victory and the city had not yet been subjected to the full sufferings of war.

Pericles was then called upon to give a funeral oration at the grave of the first Athenian casualties. In Thucydides' dramatisation Athens' premier statesman does not deliver a lament; rather his speech is a defiant rallying call in which he praises the Athenian dead by praising their city. He lists numerous points of comparison in which Athens is superior to other Greek states. 'In the first place', he explains, 'we throw our city open to all the world and we never debar anyone from learning or seeing anything which an enemy might profit by observing. We place our trust not in deception but in our courage.'

Thus the leader of the world's first democracy puts the case for the open society, making a contrast with the totalitarian system of militaristic Sparta. He goes on, 'We are lovers of beauty, yet without extravagance; and lovers of wisdom without weakness . . . . In a word then', he concludes, 'I say that our city is the School of Hellas.'

The setting for Pericles' funeral oration was the *demosion sema*, the collective tomb reserved for those who had distinguished themselves in public service, which lay outside the city walls on the road that led to the open-air *gymnasium* known as the Academy. Here Pericles himself was to be interred when, in 429 BC, he succumbed to the plague that racked the war-stricken city. For the time being, however, his star was in the ascendant, together with that of Athens herself. The road near which he addressed his fellow citizens led back into the city and through the town square, up to the Acropolis. There the newly completed Parthenon stood as eloquent testimony to Athens' greatness.

Commentators on Thucydides' text are quick to point out that Pericles' oration in no way constitutes the transcript of an actual speech. Indeed, Thucydides himself tells us as much. That fact does not, however, detract from its documentary value as a statement of Athens' self-image. But, we may ask, was the image a true one? It is possible to knock some of the gilt off the golden age of Athens by pointing out all that was wrong in Athenian society, which was by no means faultless by modern standards: the economic functioning of the democracy was dependent on slavery, and the political franchise was restricted to free-born males, excluding women not only from political rights but also from virtually all powers of self-determination. There was, besides, the matter of those subject allies, who had started out after the Persian wars as a confederacy of equals, until Athens gradually usurped their independence and appropriated the funds of their treasury into her own private exchequer.

These are some of the criticisms that might be levelled against Pericles' administration and the Athenian national character. They need to be voiced, so as to guard against blind acceptance of Periclean propaganda. Thucydides, it must be remembered, makes no claims for the truth of what Pericles says. He merely offers it as the sort of thing Pericles would have said upon such an occasion. Is it justified, then, to go to the other extreme and suggest that Athens' supposed greatness was a mere sham affordable at other people's expense? The answer has to be no. The true inspiration for Athenian success was not material; there have been many before and since who have achieved less with more. Rather, it was a native genius which came to its full flowering in the generation of Phidias and Pericles.

Pericles' funeral speech seems to epitomise the era in which the Parthenon was built, and his words shine out like a glorious sunset over Athens' cultural and artistic supremacy. As the war progressed, the city began increasingly to take on the drab mantle of a tragic hero punished and degraded by divine *nemesis* as payment for excessive pride. Her ultimate defeat was thoroughly humiliating, but, unlike the Persians earlier in the century, the Spartan victors did not despoil the shrines and temples of the gods, who, after all, were worshipped in common by all Greeks. Consequently, the Parthenon survived, along with Phidias' colossal image of the goddess. Successive generations of Greeks and – when Greece fell under Roman rule, Romans too – looked back on Phidias' achievements with wonder and longing.

The afterlife of the Parthenon

Even in the Byzantine phase of Greek history the Parthenon continued to be admired. Some of the architectural sculptures were destroyed or defaced by fanatical Christians, and the statue of the Parthenos, or a later replacement of the original, was taken off as a museum piece to Constantinople, where it is thought to have been destroyed in a fire. The building largely survived, however, and its conversion into a church around AD 500 ensured it another thousand years of upkeep. Even when, in the fifteenth century, the Ottoman Turks added mainland Greece to their empire, the Parthenon survived conversion into a mosque. In 1674 Jacques Carrey, a Flemish artist in the entourage of the Marquis de Nointel, drew the building and the sculptures still extensively preserved upon it. Thirteen years later the most beautiful of all ancient buildings was in ruins.

In 1687 a Venetian army under Francesco Morosini laid siege to the Athenian Acropolis and its Turkish garrison. The Turks had a great stock of gunpowder on the citadel and decided to store it in the Parthenon. The temple was still greatly admired by western Europeans, and the Turks assumed that Morosini would not aim his bombardment directly at it. Unfortunately, it seems a deserter from the defending force gave away the Turkish secret to the Venetians and around 6.30 p.m. on 26 September a bomb ignited the gunpowder. The inevitable explosion reduced the Parthenon to a smoke-blackened carcass.

Those who visited the Acropolis after the explosion and before Lord Elgin's time will have seen very little of the frieze remaining on the building. The central part of the long sides of the temple had been blown out, and of the east porch nothing was left standing. Only on the west was the frieze left intact. Throughout the rest of the seventeenth and the eighteenth century the remains of the Parthenon stood open to the sky. Such, however, was the sanctity of the site that a mosque was erected within the old walls, on what had once been the temple floor. Fallen masonry and sculpture were quarried to rebuild the damaged homes and defences of the small Turkish community who occupied the citadel of the much diminished city of Athens. Foreign travellers to the site broke off pieces of the sculpture to take away with them as souvenirs. This was the situation which Elgin's men found on the Acropolis when, at the beginning of the nineteenth century, they set about gathering together the battered remains of the frieze, pediment and metope sculptures for transport to England.

5 Engraving showing the explosion of the Parthenon in 1687.

2 The Frieze and its Subject

The architectural setting

The architectural setting of the frieze imposed certain constraints on its design, and we may therefore begin by examining its relationship with the building. The modern spectator enjoys a privileged view of the sculpture displayed at eye level in the dignified surroundings of a museum gallery. In antiquity the view was somewhat complicated by the frieze's position on the temple. It was external and therefore visible to spectators standing outside the building, but was partly masked by the columns of the peristyle and so could not be viewed as a continuous sequence. On the long axis it was seen high up on the wall of the temple, under the coffered ceiling sheltering the colonnaded walkway running around all four sides of the building. The situation on the short sides was complicated by the presence of a porch consisting of an inner row of six columns. Here the frieze was not placed on the wall of the temple, but above the porch, at the same level, 40 feet (12 m) off the ground. The spectator was forced to look up at a sharp angle, and then the sculpture could only be seen in snatches between the columns of the peristyle. In this position it must have been relatively inconspicuous, even allowing for the fact that figures were distinguished by added paint and illuminated by means of light reflected from below. It is perhaps not surprising, therefore, that no ancient author makes reference to it. Pausanias, who visited the Acropolis in the second century AD, notes in passing the pedimental sculptures in the gables of the temple and describes in more detail the colossal statue of Athena which stood within. Not a mention, however, is made of the frieze.

One scholar has recently attempted to see some virtue in the position of the frieze by emphasising the spectator's role in 'continuously creating new views' as he himself 'processes' around the flanks of the building: 'The viewer is thus involved in the creation of the frieze in a way that

1, 6

COL. PL. II

6 Drawing showing the frieze on the short and long sides of the Parthenon.

7 Reconstruction of the view looking eastwards out of the Propylaea. The Parthenon is seen on the right, partly obscured by the roof of the east side of the sanctuary of Artemis Brauronia. To the left is the colossal bronze statue of Athena Promachos by Phidias, and, on the far left, the Erechtheum.

s/he would not be if the frieze were not so "perversely" placed.' This shows a tendency to treat the ancient spectator as if he were able to circulate around the Parthenon as we ourselves might walk around a scale model or, indeed, the interior space of the British Museum gallery. By the fourth century BC, at least, the view from the Propylaea gateway had been obscured by a complex of buildings erected in front of the west façade of the Parthenon. That uplift of the spirit we feel today when, emerging through the narrow confines of the Propylaea, we confront the Parthenon towering over the open space of the Acropolis, was not a part of the ancient experience. The ancient approach was an oblique one, skirting the northern perimeter walls of the sanctuary of Artemis Brauronia and the open court which lay to the west of the Parthenon, both enclosures being entered through narrow gateways. A glance at a plan of the Acropolis will show how the visitor was ushered into a narrow defile running along the northern flank of the Parthenon, this being the route taken by the processions accompanying the sacrificial victims destined for the great altar situated at the far end of the Acropolis. Many must have missed the west frieze altogether; only on passing the north-west corner is the perceptive spectator likely to have caught sight of it, partially hidden behind the line of columns. A better view was to be had by entering the west court of the Parthenon and mounting the steps to stand on the terrace immediately below the west façade. This western terrace formed part of the platform on which the Parthenon was built, and on all sides of the temple this platform provided the best position for seeing the frieze.

COL. PL. IV

The ancient viewpoint was thus a restricted one, and it is curious to reflect that, since its removal from the building, the frieze is better seen and probably more admired today than ever it was in antiquity. The extraordinary refinement and subtlety of its design must inevitably provoke surprise at the apparent awkwardness of the original setting. Nevertheless, it is important always to remember that, while the frieze may be seen today as an independent work of art, it was originally part of an architectural whole. Perhaps the best way to account for this paradox is to view the frieze as a vast votive relief. Sculpture of this kind was normally carved with some scene of worship and set up in the shrine of the deity concerned. The frieze of the Parthenon may be seen as such a votive relief, but instead of being fixed to a wall, it forms a part of the fabric of the building itself.

Style and execution

It is clear that the Parthenon frieze is the product of a single design by a superior intellect, and this, it may be assumed, was Phidias. He is unlikely to have undertaken any of the actual carving: this will have been assigned to a team of stone-carvers, none of whose names have come down to us but whose different hands can be detected by comparing their subtly varying manner of treating a fall of drapery, a horse's mane or the head of a youth. Laying aside such distinctions, however, the frieze exhibits overall a remarkable degree of artistic uniformity, with its seemingly effortless naturalism appearing to grow organically out of the stone. This illusion was not achieved without careful planning and control.

9 a–d

The stylistic disparity which is often remarked upon in the metopes is missing in the frieze, and there may be a historical reason for this. The

Parthenos was dedicated in 438 BC and the roof must have been in place by then. This means, in turn, that the metopes of the Doric frieze, forming part of the entablature supporting the roof, had also to be in place. These will have been carved on the ground and afterwards hoisted into position on the building. It has been argued that the frieze blocks were also carved on the ground and subsequently fixed in place, but the likeliest scenario is that they were executed *in situ*. The blocks of stone into which the frieze was carved must have been placed by 438 BC, but the frieze itself was not necessarily carved then. The carving could have been done in time for the dedication ceremony of 438 BC, but it could equally have been carried out after the main building was finished, when the sculptors could work from their scaffold unhindered. While one team of carvers was busy with the frieze, another was perhaps cutting the pedimental sculptures for the two gable ends. The frieze and pediment sculptures are distinguished from the metopes by their stylistic unity, suggesting that the teams of carvers had by then worked together long enough for the unmistakable Parthenon style to develop. We need only compare the faces of the human participants in the frieze procession to see how closely they resemble one another. In the metopes, by contrast, there is far greater variety.

Such uniformity of facial types is in part attributable to the distance at which the frieze was to be viewed, which did not allow for recognition of greater differentiation. It has also been suggested that the style of the frieze carries a political message and that the relative sameness of the human heads is a democratic device portraying the civic community of Athens as a peer group of like-minded individuals united under Pericles' leadership. This too clever argument disregards the prevailing convention of Greek art at this time, which tended, even when representing a specific individual, to create an idealised type rather than a realistic portrait. This convention, moreover, is not limited to art produced by democratic societies and goes back in Athens itself to the archaic period, the rule of the Pisistratid tyrants and beyond.

The frieze belongs, therefore, in an artistic tradition and should be viewed as a product of generations of experimentation. Nevertheless, in its remarkable, almost breathing, vitality we can detect a distinctive hallmark which is attributable to the inspiration of Phidias' genius on the craftsmen responsible. Assuming that it was begun after 438 BC, the frieze was

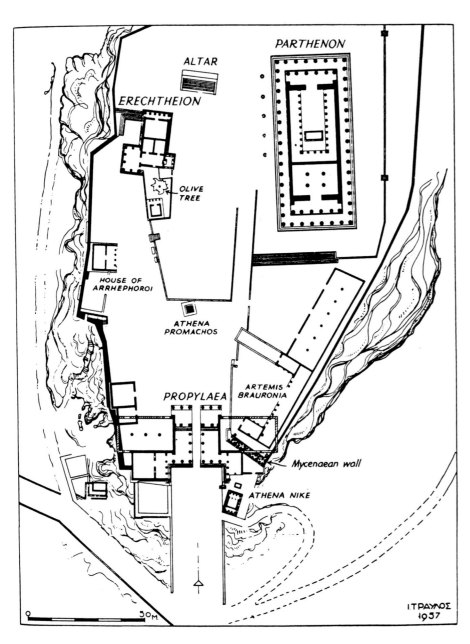

8 Plan of the Acropolis around 400 BC.

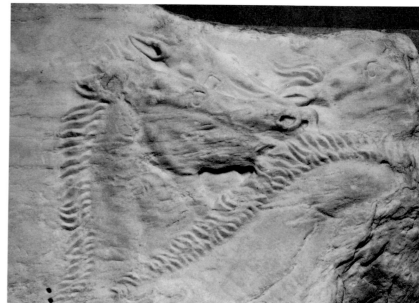

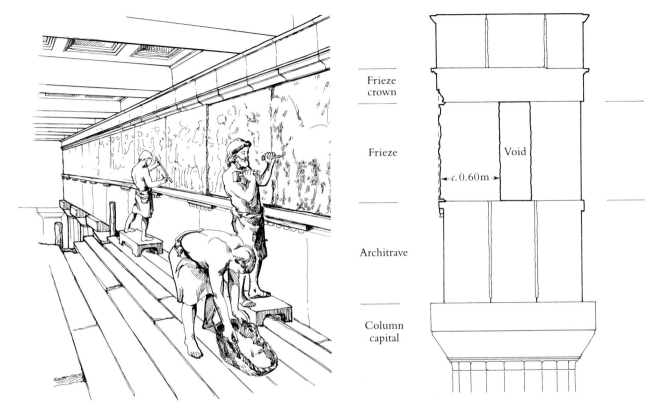

(*Left, top*)
9a–b Horsemen from separate groups of riders on the south frieze. Compare the distinctive treatment of the features of the human figures, and the difference in the rendering of the horses' manes. Two different craftsmen seem to have been responsible.

(*Left, bottom*)
9c–d Horses from two different phases of the south frieze. The similarity in the treatment of the manes suggests both groups were carved by the same hand.

(*Right*)
10 The frieze being carved *in situ* and (*far right*) the entablature, showing the frieze in section.

Frieze crown

Frieze

Void

←*c.*0.60m→

Architrave

Column capital

probably completed by 432 BC, when the surviving building accounts (inscribed on stone) suggest the pediment sculptures were also finished. Upon completion it represented the largest single example of carving in bas-relief to be found in mainland Greece and, not surprisingly, did much to popularise the artistic genre. Around 430 BC the cemeteries of Attica began to sprout grave stelae, which show an obvious stylistic affinity with the frieze. It should not be surprising that the bereaved wished to memorialise their loved ones with tombstones emulating its quiet dignity. The impulse to do so, however, may have come from the craftsmen themselves, for after completing their work on the Parthenon many will have needed other employment. They found it in the revival of a type of tomb monument which had not been seen in Athens since the Persian invasion, two generations earlier.

The subject and its arrangement

The frieze represents a procession arranged in two unequal parts. One branch began at the south-west corner and ran along the west side, turning the corner onto the north. From here it ran along the long north side until it reached the north-east corner; then, turning onto the east side of the temple, it occupied just under half of the east frieze. The other branch also began at the south-west corner, but was shorter, occupying only the south side of the frieze and, again, just under half of the east. The reason for the twin-flow arrangement of the frieze is plain to see from the plan of the Acropolis. A visitor to the Parthenon approached the west side of the temple first, where the door led into the smaller chamber which served as a treasury. There was no access into the main

8

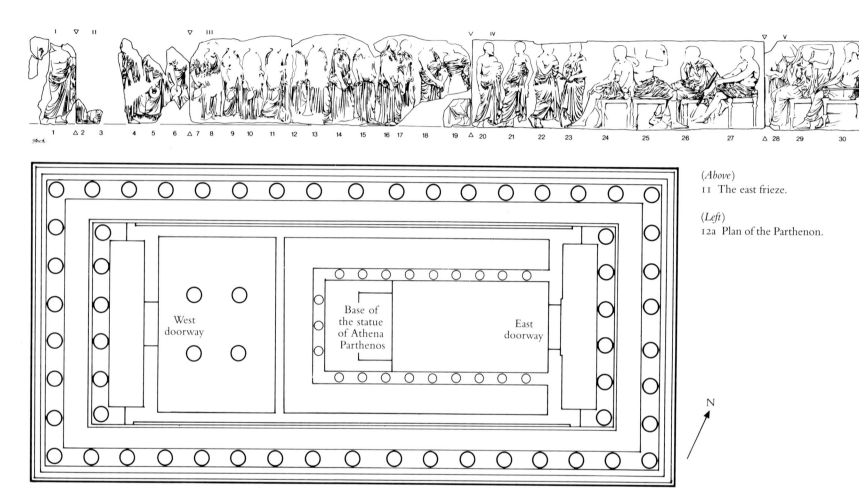

room from here and, in order to get to the door giving entrance to the room with the statue, it was necessary to walk the length of the building and approach from the east. The path skirted the shaded north side and was that used by the festival processions accompanying the victims on their way to the great altar situated towards the east side of the Acropolis. This route provided the principal view of the frieze, and the northern branch was the most important. By dividing the frieze into two, Phidias was able to determine the directional route of the procession represented on the long sides, whether on the north or the south, as being from west

to east. The idealised procession represented in the frieze could be seen as accompanying the festival pomp of real life, moving in the same direction. 'In the contemplation of the frieze', writes Philipp Fehl, 'the source of animation is the locomotion of the spectator.'

The two branches of the frieze present a procession composed of various groups of figures arranged in sequence. On the west side we see horsemen, some paired, others shown singly. The directional flow is from right to left, or south to north, but some figures, especially towards the south end, turn towards the south and thereby serve to remind us of the

12a–b

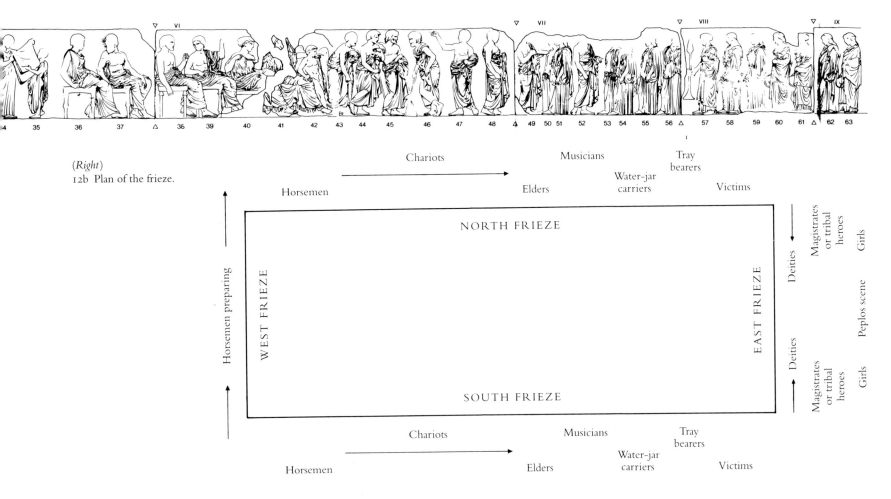

4   35   36   37   36   39   40   41   42   43   44   45   46   47   48   49   50   51   52   53   54   55   56   57   58   59   60   61   62   63

(*Right*)
12b Plan of the frieze.

parallel procession on that side. The long north side carries forward the cavalcade begun on the west, and the horsemen occupy nearly half of the total number of slabs. Ahead of them come chariots, then groups of figures walking in procession, including elders, musicians, pitcher-bearers, tray-bearers and figures leading cattle and sheep as sacrificial victims. Turning the corner onto the east side we find the female sex represented for the first time in the frieze, with a procession of girls carrying vessels for pouring ritual libations. They are met by marshals at the head of the procession and ahead of them are grouped the non-processional figures.

First, there are male figures leaning on staves and engaged in conversation. Their identification is problematic: they have been seen as the heroes of Attica, who gave their names to the ten Athenian tribes, as magistrates, or as officials (*athlothetai*) responsible for organising the festival. Ahead of them are shown the gods, whose seated pose allows them to appear larger than the mortal figures in the frieze. They are divided into two groups, one facing north to receive the procession from that side, the other south. The southern branch of the frieze follows a pattern similar to that of the north. The two processions do not actually meet, since the gods are

23

placed between them. The two groups of gods are themselves separated by five standing figures, two adults and two girls and a boy, who together participate in a ritual involving a folded cloth. This is generally thought to be the *peplos*, a garment woven anew every four years for the statue of Athena Polias.

The Panathenaic festival

The dedication of the *peplos* formed the culminating event of the festival known as the Great Panathenaia. A procession accompanied the robe up to the Acropolis on 28 Hekatombaion, the first month in the Athenian calendar, bridging our own July and August. The festival celebrated Athena's birthday, when special honours were paid to the ancient image of the city goddess on the Acropolis. Athena's statue is not shown on the frieze; instead she appears in person, seated among the other gods. As its name implies (*pan* = all), the festival brought together all sections of the city's community: old and young, male and female, citizen and foreign resident worker. All attended the sacrifices and shared in the feast of roasted meat. The procession accompanied the sacrificial victims and the new robe through the city and up to the Acropolis.

The Great Panathenaia, held every four years, was a more splendid version of an annual festival. The yearly event had been celebrated from time immemorial, but the inception of the Great Panathenaia probably dates to the year 566 BC and the rule of Athens by the tyrant Pisistratus. Like other tyrants, Pisistratus had a talent for propaganda and saw an opportunity to increase his own prestige and that of the city by re-organising its principal holiday along the lines of the major panhellenic festivals held every four years at Olympia and Delphi. There were competitions in music and athletics, and the victors were awarded olive oil in jars especially designed for the purpose. One side of the vessel carried a picture of the goddess, the other side showed the event for which the prize was given. An event in the games was the so-called *apobates* race, involving four-horse chariots ridden by a driver in a long flowing tunic

13 A Panathenaic amphora made around the time of Pisistratus' reorganisation of the festival, about 560 BC. The inscription reads, 'I am one of the prizes from Athens'. British Museum (B 130).

and a foot soldier in full armour. The chariots charged at speed to a marker, on reaching which they pulled up to allow the foot soldier to leap down. He then ran to a finishing line, and the first to cross it was declared the winner. This is thought to be the event shown in the chariot sequence of the frieze ahead of the cavalcade.

It is natural to conclude from the presence of the *peplos* on the east frieze that the whole composition represents the procession of the Great Panathenaia. Some scholars are reluctant, however, to accept this assumption. It was after all highly unusual, if not unique, for a temple frieze to depart from the normal practice of taking themes from mythology for its decorative sculpture. Elsewhere on the Parthenon this convention is observed, but in the frieze, where we might expect to see mythological characters, we seem to find instead a generalised portrayal of the contemporary Athenian community.

Scholars who have difficulty in accepting the notion of an event drawn from the civic and religious life of Athens being shown on a temple are quick to point out the discrepancies between what literary sources say about the Panathenaic procession and the event supposedly represented by the frieze. A number of elements appear to be missing, including the ranks of foot soldiers said to have marched in the parade and the girls carrying baskets and water-jars. Instead of foot soldiers there are horsemen, and the bearers of water-jars are male instead of female. Perhaps most noticeable is the absence of the ship-cart, with its mast on which the *peplos* is said to have been hoisted like a sail as it moved on rollers through the city. If the Athenians were aiming at a literal rendering of the procession, so the argument goes, surely they would have included this most characteristic of all Panathenaic emblems.

One scholar has sought to explain the absence of the ship by arguing – through a close reading of the ancient literary sources – for an annual *peplos*, in addition to the quadrennial dedication. The robe shown on the frieze of the Parthenon is thought to be too small to have been displayed 'like a sail' upon the mast of a ship. The ship, moreover, is said to be absent from those literary sources which are thought to refer to an annual Panathenaic *peplos*; hence its omission from the frieze.

Others have sought to resolve this and other discrepancies between the literary sources and the frieze by seeing it as a generalised rather than an actual rendering of the Panathenaia. Horsemen may, indeed, have accompanied the procession for a part of the way from the Dipylon Gate, where it began, to the foot of the Acropolis, but viewing the frieze as an ideal representation, transcending the actual event, there is no obligation to justify their presence. The chariots, again, may have had their part in the procession, although certainly not in violent motion as shown on the frieze. The races may have taken place along the route of the procession, but probably not simultaneously, and perhaps not even on the same day. Nevertheless, the *apobates* race was an event closely bound up with the cultural and religious values embodied in the festival, and when the frieze is viewed as an epitome of both procession and festival, then the chariots have their place in it.

Other interpretations

The frieze can thus be explained as 'an ideal embodiment of a recurrent festival'. For some, however, even this does not go far enough to bring the subject within the usual range of architectural sculpture. Much ink has been expended on elaborating new and often complex theories as to the true meaning of the frieze. Some have taken the drastic step of abandoning altogether the supposed association with the Panathenaia, while others seek an explanation in an exceptional form of Panathenaia. The main theories may be divided into three categories: mythological, symbolic and quasi-historical.

The first approach sees the frieze not as representing an idealised contemporary Panathenaia, but as the original celebration of the festival founded by the legendary Erichthonius, also known as Erechtheus. The all-important central group of figures is identified with the legendary royal household of Athens and the child E35 is seen as Erichthonius/Erechtheus handing over the very first *peplos* dedicated to Athena. This view has not found many followers, chiefly because it involves too elaborate a system of identifying individual figures elsewhere in the frieze with specific mythological persons, the same hero sometimes appearing more than once. It has also been objected that the theme of the frieze is taken 'not from myth but from cult'. In reply to this, however, it must be said that in ancient Greece the distinction between these two was not as clear-cut as this analysis implies, and the frieze may have an intrinsic ambiguity, a point to which we shall return in Chapter 4.

An alternative to the mythological is the symbolic approach. Here the Panathenaia is rejected in favour of a non-specific pageant symbolising the restoration of archaic dedications on the Acropolis destroyed by the Persian sack of Athens in 479 BC. The *peplos* is explained not as a specific Panathenaic offering, but as a token of the historical wealth of the ancient sanctuary. The chief fault of this interpretation is its failure satisfactorily to identify supposed archaic dedications in the various phases of the frieze. The objects carried by figures in the procession seem to signify actual cult paraphernalia, rather than notional votive dedications.

Variants of the symbolic approach attempt to deal with the apparent uniqueness of the frieze in Greek art by invoking assumed parallels in the art of Persia itself. The sculpted façades of the palace complexes of the Achaemenid kings at Persepolis are seen to provide the inspiration for the Parthenon frieze. The symbolic message of the frieze focuses upon the Athens of Pericles' own day: Athens, according to the argument, is presenting herself as the new mistress of the Aegean and of the Asiatic Greeks, whom she has liberated from the Persian yoke. Persian imperial propaganda is thus appropriated and adapted by neo-imperialist Athens for the purposes of promoting her own self-image. Points of comparison, however, between the Athenian and Persian reliefs are very superficial and it must be a source of embarrassment to such a notion that Athens' tribute-paying subjects cannot be identified in the frieze.

Third is the historical interpretation which, in contrast to the symbolic view, would see the frieze as evoking a very specific event, the Great Panathenaia celebrated by the Athenian community shortly before the Battle of Marathon in 490 BC. This was the contest during the war against Persia in which the Athenians, with the help of only one other city state, Plataea, saved the freedom of mainland Greece from oriental tyranny. It has been argued that the purpose of the frieze is to celebrate the heroisation of those who fell at Marathon by showing them participating in the festival prior to the battle. They are shown on horseback, or riding in chariots, even though in real life they were infantrymen, in order to indicate their status in the afterlife. The exclusion of the foot soldiers, who normally played a prominent role in the procession, is thus explained. It is further claimed that the horsemen and selected figures in the chariot sequence may be counted as 192, the very number of heroes who fell at Marathon.

Altogether, this is an ingenious interpretation, which answers objections to seeing a contemporary event on a religious building by setting the frieze in the historical past and incorporating it into the repertoire of images celebrating the cult of heroes. It also meshes well with the generally accepted view that the Parthenon as a whole commemorates Athens' part in victory over the Persians. More specifically, the battle scenes in the metopes and on the statue of Athena itself have been seen as allegories of the contest between Greeks and Persians. It solves some problems, therefore, but raises others. Not least is the count of 192 which, if true, would be the most sensational part of the argument. It was based, however, on an already discredited reconstruction of a fragmentary frieze, contradicted by the sequence of blocks assembled in the second part of this book. The count of figures, moreover, depends on too selective a reckoning, which excludes the charioteers but includes the marshals and grooms. It is not clear why the charioteers should not be included; they of all the figures in the cavalcade appear the most heroic in their long archaic tunics. If we are prepared to omit them, there seems no justification for including the marshals and grooms, who may be seen as incidental.

Time and place

These then are the principal approaches taken by scholars in recent years towards interpreting the message of the frieze. One of the questions frequently asked in the course of such speculation is whether or not the frieze represents a unity of time and place. Some argue that such a unity does exist and that the frieze portrays a particular moment in the procession. Others take the opposite view and see it as a series of independent episodes representing events happening in different places, perhaps even at different times. Such is the degree to which no stone on the frieze has literally been left unturned that in 1961 Philipp Fehl published a long article entitled 'Rocks on the Parthenon frieze'. In this, he sought to show how the rocks that frequently appear in the path of the participants in the procession mark the various stretches of the Panathenaic Way, from the stony outskirts of the city, through the level ground of the mid-city to the steep and uneven terrain of the Acropolis itself.

Fehl's conclusions were more far-reaching than the somewhat unprom-

COL. PL. III

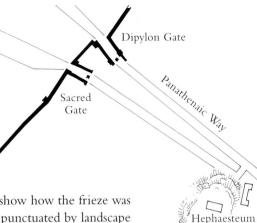

14 Plan showing the route of the Panathenaic procession from the Dipylon Gate, through the *agora* to the Acropolis, around 400 BC.

ising title of his essay suggests, his aim being to show how the frieze was composed out of a series of individual episodes punctuated by landscape elements. These show the frieze in snatches which, when taken together, cover the whole route from the Dipylon Gate, in the outer city, to the Acropolis at its heart. The frieze does not attempt to describe every step of the actual procession, but the distance it traversed is represented by a series of interconnected passages. Each forms an independent episode, artfully linked by figures or groups of figures calculated to make the transition from one phase to the next. The west frieze, with its scenes of preparation, represents the early stages at the outer limits of the city; the east side shows the head of the parade newly arrived on the Acropolis and waiting for the sacrifices to begin. There is, therefore, no literal unity of time and place. We should think instead of the procession telescoped into 'frieze time' and 'frieze space'.

Others see it differently, arguing that the frieze shows the procession at some specific, or at least restricted, time and place. The presence of the cavalcade would suggest that this was fairly early in the proceedings since, by the time the procession had reached the slopes of the Acropolis, owing to the steepness of the terrain, the horses would have had to drop out. It is suggested, therefore, that the action of the frieze is centred on the market-place (*agora*). Here the ground was open and level, allowing for the chariot races and horse parades; here stood a monument to the eponymous heroes (figures from Athens' legendary past who gave their names to the ten tribes of Attica), who are perhaps shown on the east frieze; it was here too that the altar to the twelve gods, who are also shown on the east frieze, was located. Finally, it is suggested that the *peplos*

was woven here. Rather than see the central scene of the east frieze as the dedication of the *peplos*, some scholars have viewed it as the handing over of the robe to a cult official after it had been taken from the loom. One scholar has even gone so far as to argue that the official receiving the robe is in the process of testing its quality before finally approving it.

The arguments for locating the action of the frieze in the *agora* are plausible and should not be lightly dismissed. They depend ultimately, however, on a blend of circumstantial evidence and conjecture, which gives rise to a number of possible objections. There is no hard evidence, for example, to show that the *peplos* was woven in the *agora*, whereas there are indications that this was done on the Acropolis. Here two girls known as *arrephoroi* are said to have spent the best part of a year in the service of Athena Polias. One of their official duties was to assist in setting up the warp on the loom, and a votive relief from the Acropolis appears to show this very act. In any event, so isolated is the central scene of the east frieze, sandwiched between the gods, that it seems perverse to insist upon a unity of time and place between it and the main procession. The central scene has its own particular message which, as we shall see, is lost by those who try to subordinate it to the action of the main frieze.

As for the other arguments, it is by no means certain that the chariot races took place in the city or even on the same day as the procession. They may well have formed a part of the athletic events that were held on open ground beyond the city walls on days other than that of the procession. On the matter of the eponymous heroes, although a monument to them stood in the *agora* at a later period, there is no certainty that it had been erected by the time the frieze was carved. It is even doubtful whether the two groups of male figures lounging on either side of the gods should be seen as heroes, and there is an argument for their being seen as mortal magistrates.

Two processions?

Ultimately, the case for locating the main action of the frieze in the *agora* remains unconvincing, and it seems more likely that a procession to the Acropolis, adorning a building on the Acropolis, should be shown arriving there. Some scholars who share this view have even sought a more precise definition of where on the sacred citadel the front of the procession should be located. It has been suggested that the figures walking ahead of the chariots should be seen as more than just part of a generic Panathenaic procession, and that we see here the sacrificial procession regrouped on the Acropolis in order to lead the victims to the altar. The question then arises, since the frieze is divided north and south, whether two separate sacrifices are implied. It is seen as significant that sheep occur only among the victims of the north side. Literary evidence is invoked to show that the sheep were intended for Pandrosus, the daughter of the legendary

15 Votive relief from the Athenian Acropolis, perhaps showing one of the *arrephoroi* (left) setting up the warp for weaving the sacred *peplos* on a loom.

king Kekrops, who had her own sacred precinct on the north side of the Acropolis. Pandrosus did not have her own altar, but shared that of Athena Polias. The procession on the north side of the Parthenon frieze, according to the argument, shows four sheep for Pandrosus and four cattle for Athena Polias. On the south frieze the procession is seen as accompanying a separate sacrifice of ten cattle, not this time for Athena Polias, the ancient goddess of the city, but for Athena Parthenos, the goddess of democratic Athens.

This view has already been challenged by the observation regarding Pandrosus that the sacred law referred to by Philochorus (*fl. c.* 306–260 BC) signifies sacrifices by individuals rather than state occasions such as the Panathenaia. More seriously, it assumes that there was a cult of Athena Parthenos on the Acropolis which, as we have already seen, is doubtful at the time when the frieze was carved. Viewing the frieze as two separate sacrificial processions tends in any case to obscure its essential identity as a work of art, for not only are the pedestrian groups of figures divided into two, but so are the chariots and the cavalcade. The compositional effect is to create a sense of climax as the spectator moves from the west to the east side of the building. The dramatic advantage of this device is self-evident when we consider the alternative, namely to wrap the procession in a continuous band around the temple, beginning and ending at one corner. There is, moreover, one figure on the north side of the east frieze (E47) whose gesture seems to defy the notion of two separate sacrifices. This is the marshal who turns his back on the procession immediately under his charge to beckon across the intervening gods to the procession on the south side. This act alone suggests that the two branches of the frieze should be read as one procession, accompanying one sacrifice.

Secret messages?

These, then, are some of the questions raised in the many attempts that scholars have made to explain the frieze of the Parthenon. A supposition common to all is that it has a specific message, and many treat the frieze as if it were a puzzle. Like the Theban Sphinx it guards a secret: he who solves the riddle has the answer. The frieze is thought to carry its message in code, and interpretation becomes an exercise in code-cracking. The

hope has been expressed that one day a stone inscription or papyrus text will be found to explain it. Meanwhile, all too often, scholars are to be found bending the frieze to fit a theory and then pronouncing a panegyric on Phidias' hidden meaning.

The method is exemplified in a recent proposal which comes from a reading of a papyrus preserving a fragment of the *Erechtheus*, an otherwise lost play by Euripides. The papyrus describes the sacrifice of the daughter of Erechtheus, legendary king of Athens: in accordance with a Delphic oracle, she was to give her life in order to safeguard her city against an attack by Eumolpus, king of Thrace. The cloth shown at the centre of the east frieze, it is asserted, is not the Panathenaic *peplos* but the shroud of death which the small child (E35) is about to put on. The man with her is said to be her father, Erechtheus. To the left her sisters are carrying their own shrouds in fulfilment of the pledge that if one should die, all would die. The horsemen and chariots on the long north and south sides of the frieze are explained as the military forces of Athens being martialled to defend their city.

This unlikely scenario raises more problems than it solves: the real victims of the frieze are the cattle of the north and south sides and it is their procession to the altar that provides the reason for the company of figures walking fore and aft; the chariot groups and the horsemen are not armed for war but are shown in peaceful parade; the supposed girl of the central scene of the east frieze is, as will be argued in Chapter 4, most probably a boy; we are asked to see in the broken object carried in the left hand of figure E31 a box containing the sacrificial implement. This is unlikely: the object – in spite of the damage – has been rightly identified as a footstool. The cushion-like objects on these stools carried on the heads of E31 and 32, which exhibit no fold lines, cannot be explained away as shrouds, nor the stools as 'tables of sacrifice'.

Numbers

Some have sought the clue to decipherment in numbers. Apart from the suggestion that 192 heroes of the battle at Marathon be sought among the figures of the cavalcade, it has been pointed out that while figures on the north side tend to fall into groups of four, or numbers divisible by four, on the south there is a frequency of the number ten. Thus, for example, on the north there are four cows, four sheep, four figures carrying water-jars, four pipe-players and four men playing the kithara. On the south we find ten cows, ten chariots, and the cavalcade on this side may be divided into ten ranks of six figures, each rank distinguished by its particular form of attire. One scholar has attempted an interpretation of the frieze founded on the notion of a four-fold division corresponding with the four sides of the temple. The number four has been linked to the four archaic tribal divisions of Attica; the number ten with the new division of the Athenian community into ten tribes, carried out as part of the democratic reforms of Clisthenes towards the end of the sixth century BC. The south frieze represents Periclean Athens and Athenian democracy; the north frieze shows the pre-Clisthenic city; the west represents the most ancient time when, in the legendary age of Theseus, the scattered communities of Attica were first united; the east frieze transcends all time by representing the idea of the city's periodic renewal through the image of the Panathenaic *peplos*.

The most ambitious attempt to find meaning in the numbers of figures in each phase of the procession makes the bold claim that 'every figure has a name and every number bears significance'. In order to demonstrate this hypothesis the frieze is asked to conform to the principle of division by ten or four, even when such systematic analysis seems to distort its natural syntax. While the cavalcade of the south side does fall into ten ranks of six riders, the attempt to create a parallel division of the north cavalcade is less successful. Such a view demands acceptance of an apparently arbitrary grouping of figures which does not observe natural breaks within the composition. It is, moreover, inconsistent with such a mechanistic analysis that only three and not four tray-bearers were shown on the north side. On the north side again, there is an attempt to reconstruct twelve chariots to balance ten to the south. While the number of those to the south is secure, however, on the north side the reconstruction of the chariot sequence adopted here allows for only eleven.

Sceptics might seek a different explanation for the undeniable frequency with which groups of ten or four figures recur. The frieze owes its success partly to the skill with which it has been adapted to the four sides of the building, and this design could not have been arrived at without careful thought. The recurrence of some numbers could, therefore, be attributed to the natural processes of planning involved in setting out the blueprint. Such a complete denial of the meaning of the numbers, however, perhaps errs too far in the other direction. It should be possible to find a middle way and seek a balance of form and meaning whereby some passages of the frieze may reflect numerically calculated groups of figures, while others are arranged according to artistic principles. Thus the cavalcade of the south side seems deliberately and almost monotonously arranged into equal ranks, while that of the north owes its greater appeal to the relative looseness of the composition. The attempt to reduce the north cavalcade to ten groups of six is especially forced (see pp. 98–9). Towards the eastern end of the north frieze the recurrence of the number four in the sacrificial victims, musicians and pitcher-bearers may, indeed, suggest a connection with the archaic tribes. Alternatively, we may see here a symbolic reference to the four-yearly cycle of the Panathenaia celebrated annually and then with especial splendour at the Great Panathenaia every fourth year.

In the midst of so much uncertainty and controversy it is important to keep in mind the temporal and cultural gap separating us from those for whom the frieze was intended. Some may say that the distance is too great, and that we cannot hope to resurrect the authentic 'reading', while others claim (remarkably under the circumstances) to know exactly what secret message is encoded in the frieze. In the next chapter I shall attempt a reading which, being neither too despairing nor too ambitious of finding an ultimate solution, will endeavour to interpret the frieze according to a different principle.

3 A Poem in Stone

The frieze as symphonic poem

Earlier this century the German scholar Carl Robert used the musical image of a symphony to express his perception of the artistic properties of the frieze. Writing specifically of the gods of the east frieze, he remarked upon how different compositional elements were bound together like the harmonic blending of symphonic motifs. The musical analogy can be extended to the frieze as a whole, where we see Phidias building up his composition by the subtle interplay of variation, on the one hand, and repetition on the other. The transition between one phase of the procession and another, for example, is achieved by deliberate use of pictorial devices comparable with the variation of a recurring theme within a symphonic structure. The commentary on the frieze in the second part of this book describes these in detail, but just one instance may be mentioned here: the cavalcade of the north frieze begins with a brief reminder of the principal subject of the west, namely a scene of preparation, where a boy helps an older companion to dress before mounting. The nervous backward glance and gesturing left arm of the figure waiting ahead (N133) picks up an echo of the backward look of the figure at the end of the west frieze (W2), and the backward glance is a motif used periodically throughout the whole composition, either to punctuate the rhythm or, as here, at a turning point.

The symphonic metaphor could be extended still further to describe the manner in which the procession is divided. Thus it begins on the west frieze with an introductory *adagio* portraying the horsemen who are getting ready; this is followed on the north and south sides by successive *allegro* movements, the first *moderato*, the second (the chariot race) *molto*, 'at full tilt'. The fourth movement takes the form of a long, solemn *andante* made up of the procession walking in slow tempo ahead of the chariots. The music culminates in sublime fashion with an *adagio* finale as the procession on the east frieze is brought before the company of the gods.

The frieze as drama

An alternative metaphor to music is poetry. Instead of movements we may speak of stanzas; and poetry, like music, may provide a vehicle for responding to the varying rhythm, tempo and mood of the procession. The image of a poem may also provide, perhaps more readily than music, a way to articulate the manner in which the frieze carries its message. That is not to suggest the notion of some hidden and finite meaning but, rather, to propose a way of understanding the frieze within the context of the Parthenon as a whole and ultimately in the greater setting of Periclean Athens.

A form of poetry which Periclean Athens made uniquely its own is tragedy. In recent years scholars have emphasised a point sometimes missed in reading the surviving plays, namely that they were written not to be read, but for performance in the Theatre of Dionysus cut into the south slope of the Acropolis. The question the reader is urged to ask is, 'what will have seemed significant to the original audience?'. In the same way the archaeologist reflecting upon the meaning of the frieze should ask, 'what will have been significant when it was viewed through the columns of the temple, at a steep angle and at a distance of forty feet?'. The sculpture displayed in the British Museum or in photographic form is equivalent to the text of a tragedy. On the building it is seen, as it were, in performance.

It is chastening to think of the frieze in these terms, but it is not necessary to think exclusively in this way. The experience of reading Sophocles' *Oedipus Tyrannus*, for example, is as real as seeing it performed. The impression gained of the drama is very different, but that is not to say that the reader's perception is wrong. Some might say that the concentrated act of reading is closer than performance to the act of composing, and that the reader thereby gains a deeper insight into the poet's own mind. Similarly, it could be argued that viewing the frieze at eye level in a gallery is closer to the viewpoint of the sculptor or of the

COL. PL. II

privileged visitor of antiquity who, as in Alma Tadema's painting, has ascended the scaffolding to see the frieze at close quarters. It would not be reasonable to say that what was seen from this viewpoint could not be significant unless it was also visible from the ground. Emphasising the importance of performance to the understanding of tragedy leads to the danger of saying that all that matters is what the original audience might have seen. A parallel *reductio ad absurdum* for the frieze must be that only a fifth-century BC Athenian standing on the ground has a right to pronounce upon its meaning.

On this question of meaning, there is a tendency to assume that the frieze carries a single message, one which would be there for the asking if only the enquirer could be transported back into the fifth century BC to interrogate an ancient Athenian. It is possible, for example, to argue that the frieze and, indeed, the whole of the Parthenon sculptures should be seen allegorically, as a celebration of the Athenian defeat of the Persians some two generations earlier, rather as plays by Euripides dealing with the Trojan War are sometimes seen as allegorical commentaries on the contemporary struggle between Athens and Sparta. But while it may be true that Euripidean tragedy draws upon contemporary events for its impact on the audience, on the whole it seems not to dictate a single message. Like other tragic playwrights, Euripides presents *meaning* in a field of images and ideas in which the audience is invited to pause and reflect. The meaning may appear ambiguous, but the sensitive reader does not try to iron out inconsistencies, rather he accepts them as a part of the self-contradictory world of tragedy. The message, if it can be so called, of Sophoclean drama in particular is often paradox itself and the irreconcilability of the forces that govern human destiny.

The frieze as Homeric image

Tragedy provides a thought-provoking point of comparison for the Parthenon frieze. With its episodic form and human subject matter, one might even say it is a 'tragic' monument. It was not tragedy, however, but the epics of Homer that were brought to mind by the mention of Phidias' name in antiquity: Phidias himself is reported as saying that, in creating his colossal gold and ivory statue of Zeus at Olympia, he kept before his mind's eye the image of the god as portrayed by Homer. This anecdote

was taken up by later writers, such as Dio Chrysostom (AD 40 – after 112), who was interested in the relative merits of art and poetry. Art, so it was claimed, being tied to a single image did not possess the same capacity for illusion as more versatile poetry. Phidias' Zeus, for all its great size and richness, could never compete with the multi-faceted Olympian conjured up by Homer's treasury of words. Poetry, so the argument went, made use of metaphor and ambiguity. It had the power to develop narrative through time and was able to change the form and mood of its subject. If Dio had known the Parthenon frieze as well as he knew his Homer, he might have had cause to reconsider. For the frieze exhibits that very power of suggestion which Dio regarded as the preserve of poets. By his subtle use of ambiguity and skilful manipulation of time and place, Phidias surpassed the limitations of his art and raised it to the level of the sublime.

To apply the analogy of poetry to the frieze can serve to lift our perception above seeing it merely as a vast text documenting what went on at the Panathenaic festival. If the frieze does provide such a document, then it is as a poetic or creative adaptation; it is suggestive rather than descriptive. Its subject matter is telescoped so as to transcend mere visual recording. The Parthenon frieze does not describe any one Panathenaia, current, historical or mythical; rather, it suggests the idea of festival itself. As Aristotle once put it: 'Poetry is more philosophical and more intense than history, for poetry expresses the universal, history particulars.' The two specific Panathenaic references in the frieze are the chariot races and the *peplos*. These are transcended, however, by a more general representation of an ideal festival: first comes *agon*, or contest, illustrated in the chariot race but also in the horse parades, reflecting the periodic shows of inter-tribal rivalry among the Athenian cavalry; second, there is the theme of pomp, represented by the procession on foot ahead of the chariots; finally, there is sacrifice, not acted out but implied by the procession of victims. These three – contest, pomp and sacrifice – are the essential elements of Greek festival. They are not specifically Panathenaic, but the Panathenaia include them.

Even when seemingly explicit indicators of the Panathenaia do occur, such as the chariots, they need not be seen exclusively in this way. The chariot was not a usual form of transport in Athens of the fifth century BC and was readily associated with the age of heroes as portrayed in the epics of Homer. For a heroic use of the chariot we need look no further than the west pediment of the Parthenon. Here Athena and Poseidon were shown in the centre of the pediment competing for the right to preside over the territory of Athens, having been driven to the field of battle in the manner of Homeric champions. The age of heroes in Greek mythology was associated with the beginnings of civilisation, and Athena's prize-winning act in the contest was to cause the first olive tree to sprout on the Acropolis. She thus initiated the cultivation of the fruit-bearing tree that was to become so vital in the economy of Athens.

Athena was goddess of wisdom, and the chariot was another of her inventions. The chariot, moreover, was emblematic of the founding of culture by virtue of the *techne* (skill or craft) involved in the taming and harnessing of horses. These skills were especially Athena's own and were communicated to mankind through the legendary Erichthonius. He is said to have instituted the first *apobates* race in Athens. The composition of the west pediment seems to present a divine variant, in which Athena and Poseidon are shown as having alighted and then raced to the spot where each was to perform a miracle. Such a correspondence between one part of the Parthenon sculpture (the frieze) and another (the pediment) illustrates how the sum of the parts of the frieze transcends the Panathenaic festival and does not merely record a contemporary event.

The frieze as microcosm of Athenian society

If the frieze transcends the Panathenaic Festival, then it also epitomises it by encapsulating the whole community of Athens, just as the Panathenaia represented 'all Athens'. Once again a literary analogy may help. In the midst of the *Iliad*, Homer's great war epic, the poet leads his audience into a long digression on the decoration of the shield of Achilles. On it the smith-god Hephaestus works an extraordinarily rich assemblage not of divine, or especially heroic, scenes but rather episodes of remarkably ordinary human events. These are presented in a series of five tableaux, envisaged by most commentators as five concentric circles. The first or innermost circle shows the earth, heavens and the sea; the second, city life, including scenes of a marriage celebration, a law case being disputed, the siege of a city and the ambush of a herd; the third, rural life, with representations of the seasons; the fourth, a circular dance; and, finally,

the whole composition surrounded by the world-encircling Ocean. In short, the shield presents a microcosm of the Homeric world whereby the heroic battlefield is put into the context of the world as a whole. War is put into perspective and measured against scenes of peaceful agriculture, of festival and daily life.

Like the shield, the frieze presents a microcosm, not of the world but of Athens. Here is shown a cross-section of Athenian life, of beast subservient to man, and man paying homage to god. Like the shield, the frieze is bounded at its limits, not in this instance by the Heavens and the Ocean but by the boundaries of the city: at the western end the cavalcade is shown preparing to escort the procession from the Dipylon Gate piercing the perimeter wall of the city; at the eastern end, the procession arrives on the Acropolis. Thus the frieze bridges symbolically the distance between the city outskirts and its sacred heart. The final approach is carefully orchestrated as the two branches of the procession, south and north, turn the corners of the east side of the temple and converge on the centre.

It is no coincidence that, rounding the corner onto the east frieze, the spectator was suddenly presented with female figures making their first appearance in the procession. In the male-orientated society of fifth-century Athens women were excluded from the main social stream. The girls shown on the frieze, however, are in a peculiar class of their own, being past puberty but not yet married. They seem to provide a counter-point to the youthful male warriors (*ephebes*) at the other end of the procession, who are past puberty also but have not yet won full citizen status. These socially marginal groups, therefore, mark the boundaries of the frieze and, at the same time, define the physical limits of the path traversed by the procession that moved from the edge of the city to the Acropolis.

Ahead of the girls come non-processional figures: first, marshals waiting at the head of the procession, and then two groups of male figures – one to the north, the other to the south – in conversation, leaning on staves. Some would see them as effecting a cosmological transition from the mortal world of the procession to the divine realm of the gods. For these are seen as heroes and therefore half-way between the two. More particularly, they are thought to be the eponymous heroes of Athens. Others would prefer to see them, instead, as probable mortals, and they have been connected with the *archons*, magistrates who were elected annually to manage the city administration, or *athlothetai*, officials charged with managing the Panathenaia. As mortals, rather than heroes, these figures could still serve as tribal representatives, since both the *archons* and the *athlothetai* were drawn one from each tribe. Whatever their identity, the pictorial function is clearly to act as a compositional device for marking the transition between the processional phase of the frieze and the non-processional groups of seated gods.

The gods are shown seated in the manner of a grandstand audience pictured in relaxed mood before the ceremonies have begun. They are divided into two groups, one facing south and the other north to greet the procession coming from each side. The outer aisle seats are reserved on one side for Hermes and on the other for Aphrodite and the boy-god Eros. This was a clever way of bringing those gods who personified the deepest-felt of human experiences closest to the mortals of the frieze. Hermes was messenger of the gods, and one of his functions was to lead souls into the Underworld. Aphrodite, by contrast, and her son and agent Eros were the gods of love, from whose pangs even the deathless Olympians were not immune. The gods seated nearest to the centre are Zeus and his daughter Athena. Zeus is placed in this pre-eminent position by virtue of his being father of the gods, while Athena is there owing to her prestige as goddess of the city and of the temple itself. It is unclear whether the gods are resting at home on Mount Olympus or whether they should be seen as in divine epiphany on the Acropolis. The ambiguity is perhaps intentional, and here, as elsewhere in the frieze, it is unwise to force a precise definition where none may have been intended.

Between the gods is another set of figures, occupying the very centre of the east frieze. Here is shown the *peplos*, which is generally regarded as the key to understanding the whole frieze and is the principal reason for seeing it as a representation of the Panathenaic procession. So unusual is the subject of this central scene and so many are the questions it raises that it merits a chapter of its own.

4 The *Peplos* Scene

Myth or cult?

The gods of the east frieze are shown seated and larger than the processional figures, but the eye has no sooner adjusted to this change than, without apparent warning, the frieze returns to the former, mortal scale. At the very centre of the east frieze, between the gods, is a group of figures which may seem compositionally weak and disconcertingly isolated from the procession and the waiting gods. There are, however, mitigating circumstances: viewing the frieze on the building, the field of vision was narrowed at this point by the fourth and fifth column of the peristyle, which acted as a vertical frame. The picture thus formed within it consists of Hera and Zeus on the left, and, on the right, Hephaestus and Athena. The two outer deities of each pair look inwards, thereby reinforcing the idea of a unified tableau, already defined by the flanking columns.

There have been many attempts to interpret this central scene, and here at least the viewer may expect a more than merely generalised explanation. The subject seems to represent some specific ritual involving five persons, two adults and three children. From left to right appear two adolescent girls, bearing on their heads what most scholars agree to see as cushioned stools. The hindmost carries a much damaged but still recognisable footstool on her left arm. They are met by a full-grown woman who assists the leading girl with her burden. She stands back to back with a man whose long ungirt tunic may be recognised as a priest's garb. He is confronted by a younger child and between them they support a folded cloth usually identified as the Panathenaic *peplos*. There is doubt as to whether the group is meant to be seen as mortals undertaking some contemporary ritual of Athenian cult, or as legendary figures of the heroic past, perhaps engaged in the first such ritual. There is much scholarly disagreement, and even the sex of the child (E35), traditionally regarded as male, has been disputed. A comparison has been made with the figure carved on a grave stele in New York, where a young girl wears an ungirt *peplos*. There is no certainty, however, that the dress of figure 35 is a *peplos*;

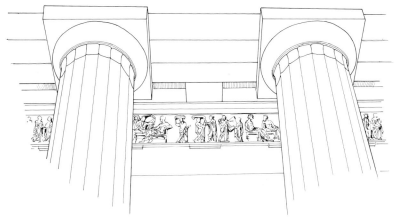

16 View through the columns framing the central scene of the east frieze.

an alternative identification is suggested by another grave stele in Thebes Museum, where a youth in a strikingly similar pose is shown wearing a *chlamys*. This is a form of cloak pinned on one shoulder and worn exclusively by males. The pose and the dress of the child on the frieze, moreover, are similar to those of a figure of the legendary Erichthonius on a fragmentary cup in the Acropolis Museum.

The most popular identification of the figures in this central scene of the frieze is as cult officials of Athena. Thus the two girls (E31–2) are often seen as *arrephoroi*, girls between the ages of seven and eleven who were dedicated for part of the year to the service of Athena on the Acropolis. The woman (E33) is seen as the priestess of Athena Polias; the man as the *archon basileus*, chief magistrate and overseer of Athenian state religion. The suggestion that E35 is a girl has not found general agreement; if identified as a boy, he may be a temple-server, like Ion in Euripides' tragedy of that name, who served in the temple of Apollo at Delphi.

Although the central scene appears to portray a cult activity, which would have been intelligible to contemporary Athenians, there is no need to see it exclusively in terms of cult. Little support has been found for the suggestion that the scene portrays the legendary royal household of Athens, comprising King Kekrops, his three daughters and his successor the earth-born Erichthonius/Erechtheus. Most scholars have sought an answer to the problem without resort to myth, but Walter Burkert has shown how close is the correlation between the rites surrounding the

(*Right*)
17 Grave stele showing a girl in an ungirt *peplos*. Made on Paros around 430 BC. New York, Metropolitan Museum of Art.

(*Above*)
18 Boeotian grave stele from Lokris showing a youth in a *chlamys*, remarkably similar to the dress of figure 35 on the east frieze. Made around 400 BC and now in Thebes Museum.

arrephoroi and the myth of the daughters of Kekrops. He has sought to demonstrate how the ritual effectively dramatised the myth, and in the light of this we may adopt a reading of the frieze which, while accepting the mortal status of the group as cult officials, nevertheless sees in their cult function a surrogate representation of the legendary royal household of Athens. The *arrephoroi* represent the daughters of Kekrops and, it may be conjectured, the temple-boy impersonates Erichthonius, his involvement with the *peplos* evoking the role of his mythical paradigm as founder of the first festival. Something of the kind has already been hinted at by Erika Simon but, preferring a closer family tie between the child and the priest/Kekrops figure, she has suggested Erysichthon, the son of Kekrops, for the mythical paradigm. As the offspring of the first king of Athens, Erysichthon certainly had a place among the heroic cults of the city, but he died young, achieved little of note and had no particular association with the Panathenaia or the *peplos*. Erichthonius, although not a blood

19 Fragmentary cup from the Acropolis of Athens showing Athena with the legendary Erechtheus drinking from a libation bowl. Made in Athens around 460–450 BC.

relative of Kekrops' daughters, was nevertheless linked to them by a myth and a major cult associated with it.

The myth tells how Athena entrusted to the daughters of Kekrops a basket with the warning never to open it. Curiosity got the better of them, however, and two of the girls, Aglauros and Herse, lifted the lid to look inside. There they found Erichthonius accompanied by a monstrous snake. This thinly veiled allegory of a young girl's sexual awakening ended tragically when the girls fled in terror from what they had seen and in fright fell to their deaths over the edge of the Acropolis. The daughter who had stayed true to Athena's command was Pandrosus and she remained on the Acropolis, honoured with her own shrine. This can be seen to this day in the form of a once walled enclosure stretching westwards from the Erechtheum.

The ritual dramatising the myth is described by Pausanias as follows:

Adjoining the temple of Athena is the shrine of Pandrosus, the only one of the sisters to be faithful to the trust. I was much amazed at something which is not generally known, and so I will describe the circumstances. Two maidens dwell not far from the temple of Athena Polias, called by the Athenians 'Bearers of the Sacred Offerings'. For a time they live with the goddess, but when the festival comes round they perform at night the following rites. Having placed on their heads what the priestess of Athena gives them to carry – neither she who gives nor they who carry have any knowledge what it is – the maidens descend by the natural underground passage that goes across the adjacent precincts, within the city, of Aphrodite in the Gardens. They leave down below what they carry, and receive something else which they bring back covered up. These maidens they henceforth let go free, and take up to the Acropolis others in their place.

Pausanias' account was written half a millennium after the Parthenon was built and it is surely unwise to attempt to fit his text to the frieze. The precise nature of the ritual being enacted will probably never be known, in spite of the many attempts to make sense of it. The stools with their cushions and the footstool carried in the left hand of one of the girls must, however, bear some specific meaning. Possible interpretations range from their being seen as the workstools of those responsible for weaving the sacred *peplos*, to seats for the epiphany of absent deities. Pandrosus and the Earth goddess Ge Kourotrophos have been suggested as possible recipients. This idea is linked to the suggestion that the frieze represents two sacrificial processions, one being for Pandrosus. It presupposes, however, that Pandrosus is more significant than other mythical figures who had a cult affinity with Athena Polias: Erechtheus, the legendary king of Athens, for example, enjoyed an annual sacrifice of cattle and sheep which may have formed a part of the Panathenaic celebrations. The precise function of the stools will probably never be known, but this will not deter future speculation.

Rite of passage

The search for a specific identification of the ritual being enacted in the east frieze should not be allowed to obscure the importance of the more general argument that, whatever their actions mean, these figures are to be seen as surrogates of the Athenian royal house. Taking the whole central group of the east frieze at face value, what we see are two family units: the mortal representatives of the Athenian royal family sandwiched between two parts of a divine family group. The central scene forms an independent compositional unit, and yet it cannot be entirely isolated from the rest of the frieze. Ultimately, it must provide a focal point for the whole. One of the striking features of the east frieze is the sudden appearance, after turning the corner from the north or south sides, of girls of marriageable age. Elsewhere in the procession there are no female figures, but here, at the approach to the gods, girls are shown for the first time. There can be no doubt that the Parthenon and its frieze provided a showpiece of Athenian public values, political, athletic, military and artistic. As such it may readily be identified with the world of men, but the Parthenon frieze, like the Panathenaia, also embodied female values. Athena represented both sexes, being both warrior and weaver. The Panathenaic procession and presentation of the *peplos* provided the means by which the domestic and normally private art of weaving could be brought into the public domain. The attention of the whole city was thus focused upon the female craft and its importance to human society.

The weaving of the Panathenaic *peplos* began at the autumn festival of the Chalkeia nine months before its presentation. It was woven by girls of marriageable age and women from noble Athenian families, but the weaving was initiated by the *arrephoroi* in conjunction with the priestess of Athena Polias. This function of the *arrephoroi* was significant, for Pandrosus and her sisters were credited with weaving the first woollen garment. As Burkert remarks, 'the *arrephoroi* repeat the former first begin-

ning of culture, which the daughters of Kekrops (Kekropidai) had instituted'. It is interesting to note that the specific task assigned to the *arrephoroi* is setting the warp up on the loom. This technically difficult exercise was the first and most important step in the weaving of a successful web. The first acquaintance of the *arrephoroi* with the art of weaving may be seen as an initiation rite and, indeed, the whole institution of the *arrephoria* can be regarded as a rite of passage for girls approaching the age of puberty.

The pioneering social anthropologist Arnold van Gennep has shown that rituals of this kind serve to underscore vital transitional experiences in the lives of individuals, such as birth, marriage and death, or, in this case, puberty, the onset of adolescent awareness and adult responsibilities. Rites of passage follow a regular pattern of separation from the norms of social life, followed by a period of living apart, then reincorporation into the social group. Through their sojourn on the Acropolis the *arrephoroi* were introduced, on the one hand, to the art of weaving, by which as married women they would make their chief contribution to the household economy; and on the other hand they were made symbolically aware of their role as child-producers through familiarity with the phallic snake of Erichthonius. The ritual of the *arrephoroi* was of relevance not only to their own life experience but also to the Athenian maidenhood at large. As Walter Burkert succinctly puts it, 'all Athenian girls were Kekropidai'. This is perhaps the reason for the special place afforded the girls on the frieze.

The *arrephoria* took place in Skiraphorion, the last month of the Athenian year. At the end of it, as Pausanias remarks, the two girls who had spent the year in the service of Athena were dismissed. The archons, too, laid down office at the end of the year, and the incoming magistrates were sworn in on the first day of the Panathenaic month of Hekatombaion. It must have been one of the first religious duties of the newly appointed *archon basileus* to appoint the two girls who would serve Athena on the Acropolis. Occurring at the end of the first month of the Athenian year, the Panathenaia provided the community with the first occasion on which it would see the new archonship assembled together. This may explain why, if the identification is accepted, they are figured so prominently on the frieze at the head of the procession. By the same reasoning, the recent appointment of the *arrephoroi* is celebrated in the central position that they occupy between the gods. Banished from the Acropolis at the end of the previous year, here at the first major festival of the new year the *arrephoroi* are shown returned to repeat the cycle of their initiation, both as representatives of the maidenhood of Athens and as the *dramatis personae* of a myth in which they are cast as the daughters of the legendary Kekrops.

The peplos as emblem of the cosmic order

The principal theme of the Parthenon frieze taken as a whole is the celebration of a festival where the present mingles with the heroic past and mortal seeks to communicate with divine. On the west, north and south sides the idea of festival is a general and a universal one. The various elements that go to make up the composition do not specifically represent the Panathenaic festival, although the chariots may suggest it. On the east frieze, however, the subject is more focused and relates more specifically to the Panathenaia. It is illuminating to remark how the east frieze moves from groups of anonymous girls walking in procession to groups of non-processional male figures who, although anonymous, may stand for a specific magistracy and thereby come to represent tribal divisions within the city. Ahead of them come non-processional seated figures who corporately represent the family of Olympian gods, but who, unlike the magistrates, can be identified individually. Between the gods come mortals again who, like the magistrates, may be linked anonymously with particular groups within the city, but may also be associated with specific heroic personalities. By this means the frieze is focused by degrees upon particular groups and ultimately upon individuals. In the procession the ceremonial is of a general kind: contest, pomp and sacrifice, whereas within the two groups of deities the viewer is invited to think in terms of some specific ritual.

This increasing particularisation of the east frieze centres at last on the *peplos*. It is this that gives the frieze as a whole a specific Panathenaic reference. To us this folded piece of cloth may seem a dull and somewhat insignificant image, and it is necessary to restore its ancient cultural associations. The weaving of the new robe for Athena signified the re-enactment of the making of the first woollen garment through the art invested in humankind by Athena. Like the chariot and the olive, the

peplos was an image resonant with the idea of the beginnings of culture. Further, the *peplos* was not the inanimate image it appears to be on the frieze today for, as every Athenian who saw it knew, in reality it was alive with woven scenes representing the gigantomachy, the mythical battle between gods and giants. This story, in which the rational Olympian deities secured their supremacy in the cosmos, served as yet another reminder of the origins of civilisation.

It has been asserted that the frieze does not show the quadrennial *peplos*, woven with a tapestry of the gigantomachy, but a lesser annual dedication, woven in plain purple. The argument depends upon an uncertain reading of the ancient literary sources and denies the potency of the *peplos* as a 'charged image', both in the context of the Panathenaia and in the overall iconographic programme of the Parthenon. The frieze was painted, and it is possible that some scenes of the gigantomachy were depicted in miniature on the sculpted *peplos*. If so, they will have been unintelligible from a distance of 40 feet. Instead, the ancient spectator could look to the Doric frieze of the Parthenon where, on the east side, the metopes were carved with the same mythological subject. It was surely no coincidence that of the four battle scenes chosen for the metopes of the Parthenon, that of gods and giants was selected for the same side as the representation of the *peplos* on the Ionic frieze.

In contrast to the metopes, the prevailing mood of the frieze of the Parthenon is peaceful. Where the arts of war are represented in the horsemen and chariots, they are shown as part of a peaceful parade presenting a microcosm of all Athenian society. Old men are there, girls of marriageable age, animals from the fields and magistrates in civic dress, while the gods look on as if to bestow their blessing. The violent scenes of the metopes, with their mythical battles between Greeks and Amazons, Greeks and Trojans, Lapiths and Centaurs and gods and giants, are missing from the frieze, except in the *peplos* at the very heart of the east frieze. War and strife, therefore, have their place on the frieze, just as in Homer's shield of Achilles death and destruction take their place amidst the scenes of prosperous settled society.

The *peplos* bids us look beyond the frieze to the metopes for the gigantomachy, but also further afield to the sculptures of the east pediment. The new robe was presented on the occasion of the festival celebrating Athena's birthday and the subject of the east pediment was Athena's birth.

Thus we see Athena in three aspects: first, in the pediment, released from the head of Zeus, fully grown and armed, striding out into the world; second, on one of the east metopes as divine protagonist in the gigantomachy; finally, on the frieze as one of the company of gods, passively awaiting the coming procession. On the frieze Athena is not shown as the actual recipient of the *peplos*, and many scholars have remarked that the action of the frieze is curiously incomplete. The composition culminates but does not conclude with the handling of the robe, and only with reference above and beyond the frieze does the image make sense.

Pandora

The scene of the handling of the *peplos* fell immediately over the doorway leading into the main chamber of the temple. Instead of raising the eyes to the metopes and pediment sculpture above the frieze, the ancient spectator could lower them to look through the open doorway and down the long hall stretching before him. There, shimmering in the half-light, could be made out the shape of a sculpted image, richer and more imposing than any to be seen on the outside of the building. This was the awesome colossus of Athena veneered in gold and ivory by Phidias. Decked in full armour, Athena greeted the viewer with a fixed and emotionless stare and presented a very different aspect of the goddess from that of the figure on the frieze shown seated and relaxing with her family. Here Athena is on duty and wears her helmet, from the centre of which springs a sphinx flanked by winged horses. On her breast she still wears the aegis with its badge of the manically staring gorgon. On the outside of the shield, as we have seen, and on the inside, and again around the soles of her sandals the battle rages: an Amazonomachy, a Gigantomachy and a Centauromachy echoing three of the themes of the metopes. On the base supporting the statue was to be found a quite different subject. Here, as on the east pediment, was a company of gods gathered to be present at the birth, not this time of Athena, but of the archetypal woman, Pandora.

Like that of Athena, this nativity was framed by Helios, god of the sun, on the left, and Selene, goddess of the moon, on the right. The story of Pandora, forged out of clay by Hephaestus and clothed by Athena, is told by the early Greek poet Hesiod. A summary of Hesiod's two accounts of Pandora, one in the *Theogony* and the other in the *Works and Days*, runs as follows: a sacrifice took place in the presence of gods and men, presided over by the Titan Prometheus. Prometheus set out to deceive the gods into accepting the inedible parts of the victims. Angered by this, Zeus denied man the use of fire, but Prometheus retaliated by stealing back the flame and restoring it to mankind. Zeus's reply was to give man a further gift, namely woman, of which Pandora was the prototype, constructed by Athena and Hephaestus and endowed with gifts by, among others, Hermes (the god of deceit), Peitho (persuasion) and Aphrodite, the goddess of erotic love. Both meat-sacrifice and woman are, in Hesiodic terms, a *dolos* (deceit). Prometheus' deceit in tricking Zeus into accepting the gift of the fat and bones began the feud between men and the gods. Men in return were tricked into accepting another deceit, woman, beautifully packaged but concealing an evil within.

No detailed literary or pictorial record of the statue base survives, but to judge from sketchy and summary copies of the Roman period, Pandora was rendered in a stiff automaton-like pose, visible also in a number of vase-paintings. A badly damaged but once beautiful white-ground cup of around 460 BC shows the creation of Pandora, or rather her alias Anesidora, literally, 'she who bestows gifts from below'. She stands stiff in the centre of the composition, her arms hanging down by her sides and her head turned to the left. On the right stands the smith-god Hephaestus, who places a golden crown upon her head; on the left Athena, the goddess of weaving, whose left arm reaches behind Pandora to pin the *peplos* on her shoulder. Athena wears the *aegis*, shown here as a woven shawl, patterned like a tapestry with a narrow woven border of chevrons above the snake fringe.

The appearance of this seemingly baneful figure in the sculptural programme of the Parthenon has perplexed some commentators. What purpose can be served by Hesiod's *kalon kakon*, the 'beautiful bane' and source of human suffering? She it was who lifted the lid from the jar and released the ills that forced man, who had lived hitherto like the gods, to bow his neck to the yoke of hard necessity. It is tempting to speculate whether Phidias selected the image of the making of Pandora as a mere metaphor of his own creative act in constructing a goddess. If so, it was an extraordinary conceit. Martin Robertson has suggested another explanation. He has no difficulty in accommodating Pandora in Phidias'

20

20 The creation of Pandora by Athena (left) and Hephaestus (right). Reconstruction from a white-ground cup made about 460 BC and now in the British Museum.

scheme as a token of the unpredictability of divine will and, by implication, the frailty of the human condition. This must be right, for we cannot rewrite Hesiod to suit; if the contradiction is there, then let it be accepted as a statement about the way the Greeks saw their world.

In a reflection upon the Hesiodic myth John Gould compares the world of Hesiod with that portrayed by Homer. Hesiod, we are told, 'contributes a sense of depth and perspective to the Homeric model, the awareness . . . of a dark hinterland to the Olympian scene'. The Homeric image of divinity is defined as one 'of marvellous and compelling adequacy; it underwrites and explains the human sense of contradiction and conflict in experience, and yet contains contradiction within a more fundamental order. It enables divinity to be understood as the source of disorder in the world, and, in the extreme case, mirrored in the myth of the war between gods and giants, as the ultimate defence of order against brute chaos . . . .'

The gigantomachy woven into the *peplos* of the east frieze of the Parthenon may be read in these terms. The power of the gods to defeat the giants both controls and threatens the stability of human fortune. This sinister aspect of Greek divinity is embodied in Pandora, mythical paradigm of the girls who wove Athena's *peplos*. She is the quintessential contradiction, the beautiful evil which, in Gould's evocative phrase, provides the 'dark hinterland' to the image of the divine projected elsewhere on the Parthenon.

Pandora adds a new dimension to the viewer's perception of the central scene of the east frieze and in so doing serves to complete the subject by presenting a separate image charged with pictorial, mythological and cultural echoes. There is, for example, a parallel to be drawn between the Kekropidai and Pandora: both are entrusted with something which they open – Pandora the jar that contains the evils that afflict mankind, Aglauros and Herse the basket containing the Erichthonius child. From Pandora's jar issues the male need of, and dependence upon women; the Kekropidai open the chest that reveals the Erichthonius child and the snake, symbolic of male sexuality. Before Pandora men had lived free from women, while the Kekropidai as chaste virgins represent a female society as yet unexposed to the male sex. It is not surprising that Pandora is sometimes coupled with the daughters of Kekrops in ancient literary sources. There is even evidence to suggest that Pandora had a cult on the Acropolis and received sacrifices.

Just as there are parallels to be drawn with the daughters of Kekrops, so are there with their mortal representatives. The *arrephoroi* initiate the weaving of the first *peplos*, the gift that Pandora first received from Athena. They wear white garments and gold jewellery; Hesiod refers to the silver, that is to say white, garments and gold jewellery of Pandora. The mythical archetype of the *arrephoroi* is not Pandora but the Kekropidai, and yet as the prototype of woman Pandora is a paradigm for all.

Furthermore, a comparison may be made between Pandora and Erichthonius in the extraordinary circumstances of their respective 'births'. The story of Erichthonius' conception is particularly unusual. Unable to control his lust for Athena, the smith-god Hephaestus ejaculated onto the thigh of the virgin goddess, who wiped her leg in disgust with a piece of wool. This she threw to the ground and there the divine seed mingled with the earth and was propagated. A vase-painting in Berlin shows the Earth goddess Ge delivering the child up to an expectant Athena, while Hephaestus looks on. Although he was born of the Earth, therefore,

21

Erichthonius was also a child of Athena and Hephaestus. We may note in passing that the mortal surrogate of Erichthonius in the central scene of the frieze is placed adjacent to his divine 'parents'. It is worth remarking, too, that both Pandora and Erichthonius are created from a mixture of wool and earth. Pandora is modelled from clay and draped in Athena's woollen *peplos*, while Erichthonius is born of raw wool mixed with semen thrown upon the earth. (The derivation of his name is usually given as *erion*, wool, and *cthon*, the earth.) Both Pandora and Erichthonius are the product of extraordinary but diametrically opposite acts of creation: Pandora is forged by sober *techne*, the craftsman's skill; Erichthonius, by contrast, is the child of passion. Pandora is endowed with knowledge of weaving, while Erichthonius is credited with the invention of the chariot. Thus they betoken complementary male and female roles, weaving and warriorship, the attributes that characterise the double personality of Athena herself. It is not surprising that, while Phidias adorned the base of the Parthenos with the birth of Pandora, his pupil Alkamenes portrayed the birth of Erichthonius on the base of the statues of Athena and Hephaestus housed in the Hephaesteum.

The central scene of the east frieze thus has a special meaning which provides a darker image than that of the procession. It serves, nevertheless, to give a context for the main subject of the frieze, where the people of Athens are gathered to pay homage to their gods on the occasion of the Great Panathenaic festival. The manner of representation aims not at the particular, but at a universal portrayal of the city, telescoped, as it were, into an ideal procession. We should not, therefore, be surprised that specific elements known to have been part of the procession are not included. The *peplos* scene provides an unequivocal Panathenaic context; for the rest, the frieze does not aim to document the event itself. It serves, rather, as a visual metaphor of the spirit of the Panathenaic festival, as it was conceived in Pericles' day, embodying and reinforcing the communal values of the city, but at the same time transcending it. 'When old age shall this generation waste, thou shalt remain in midst of other woe', wrote Keats of his Grecian Urn, and although the citizens of ancient Athens have long ceased to climb the Acropolis to celebrate their festival in honour of Athena, Phidias' brilliant conception still seems, in Plutarch's words, 'untouched by time'.

21 The birth of Erichthonius (*top*), on a red-figured cup attributed to the Kodros painter. Made in Athens around 425 BC and now in Berlin. The names are inscribed above the participants: from left to right, Kekrops, Ge, Erichthonius, Athena, Hephaestus, Herse.

Notes

Chapter 1 The Parthenon and Athens

The Parthenon and its sculptures

For a lucid summary of the Periclean buildings on the Acropolis see Wycherley (1978), pp. 105–54. The standard works for studying the sculptures of the Parthenon are now F. Brommer's *Die Skulpturen der Parthenon-Giebel* (Mainz 1963), *Die Metopen des Parthenon* (Mainz 1967), and *Der Parthenonfries* (Mainz 1977). For a rather dry summary in English of Brommer's monumental work see his *The Sculptures of the Parthenon* (London 1979); both more entertaining and informative is Boardman (1985). Other studies include E. Berger's monographs relating to the cast reconstructions of the Parthenon sculptures in Basel: *Die Geburt der Athena im Ostgiebel des Parthenon* (Basel 1974); *Documentation zu den Metopen* (1986). A fine survey in English of the Parthenon pediments is O. Palagia, *The Pediments of the Parthenon* (Leiden 1993). G. Despinis publishes important notes on aspects of the Parthenon sculpture in his *Parthenonia* (in Greek, Athens 1982). A. Mantis has produced a recent series of articles publishing new joins of fragments of the pediment sculptures, frieze and south metopes. The latter will eventually be brought together in a single monograph. Further studies of the Parthenon sculptures are to be found in Berger (1984) and (1988).

Parthenos and Parthenon

On the statue of Athena Parthenos see Leipen (1971); id., 'Athena Parthenos: problems of reconstruction' in Berger (1984), pp. 177–81. On a new reconstruction of the Parthenos in Nashville, Tennessee, see B. S. Ridgway, 'Parthenon and Parthenos', in *Festschrift für Jale Inan* (Istanbul 1989), pp. 295–305. Scholars have taken particular interest in the shield of the Athena Parthenos: for a recent study with bibliography see H. Meyer in *Mitteilungen des Deutschen Archäologischen Instituts, Athenische Abteilung* 102 (1987), pp. 295–321. On the absence of a cult of Athena Parthenos see C. J. Herington, *Athena Parthenos and Athena Polias – a study in the religion of Periclean Athens* (Manchester 1955). For evidence of a later cult of Athena Parthenos see Mansfield (1985), p. 153, note 8, and p. 232. It has also been suggested that the Panathenaic *peplos* (for which see below) was dedicated to the Athena Parthenos statue: see Mansfield (1985), p. 43, with bibliography and his gloss. On the images of Athena see B. S. Ridgway, 'Images of Athena on the Acropolis', in Neils (1992), pp. 119–42.

The Persian wars

For a recent study of the Peace of Callias see E. Badian in *The Journal of Hellenic Studies* 107 (1987), pp. 1–39; on the political implications of the Parthenon see R. Meiggs in *Greece and Rome*, supplement to vol. 10 (1963), pp. 36–45; Castriota (1992).

Pericles' building programme

On the monuments erected by Pericles' administration see T. L. Shear Jr, 'Studies in the early projects of the Periklean building program' (PhD dissertation, Princeton 1966); A. Corso, *Monumenti Periclei. Saggio, critico sulla attività edilizia di Pericle, Memorie, Classe di scienze morali, lettere ed arti*, 40 fasc., 1 (Venice 1986). For the four major temples of the Periclean building programme, besides the Parthenon, see Wycherley (1978), p. 69 with bibliography. On the debate in the Athenian assembly over Pericles' actions see Meiggs, op. cit. under 'The Persian wars'. For Pericles' offer to rebuild the temples at his own expense, see Plutarch, *Life of Pericles*, 14.1f.

The afterlife of the Parthenon

For the later history of the Parthenon see Le Comte de Laborde, *Athènes aux XVI et XVII Siècles*, 2 vols (Paris 1854); Korres (1990). On the explosion see C. Hadjiaslani, *Morosini, the Venetians and the Acropolis* (Athens 1987), translated into German for Korres (1990), pp. 6–16; for Lord Elgin see A. H. Smith, 'Lord Elgin and his collection', *Journal of Hellenic Studies* 36 (1916), pp. 163–372.

Chapter 2 The Frieze and its Subject

The architectural setting

On viewing the frieze between the columns of the peristyle see R. Stillwell, 'The Panathenaic frieze' in *Hesperia* 38 (1969), pp. 231–41. For the attempt to justify the placement of the frieze in terms of the spectator's role 'continuously creating new views' see Osborne (1987). On the approach to the Parthenon on the Acropolis see G. P. Stevens, 'The Periclean entrance court of the Acropolis of Athens', *Hesperia* 5 (1936), pp. 443–520; id., 'The setting of the Periclean Parthenon', *Hesperia Supplement* 3 (1940), especially pp. 4–7: 'The first good view in antiquity of the Parthenon'.

Style and execution

The most penetrating analysis of the individual sculptors responsible for the carving is Schuchhardt (1930). His estimate of up to eighty different hands is probably excessive. For a survey of other discussions see Brommer (1977), pp. 271–5. For the argument as to whether the frieze was carved in a workshop (and subsequently hoisted into place) or on the building see Brommer (1977), pp. 168–70. For the making of a convincing case for its being carved on the building see M. Korres in Berger (1988), pp. 19–27. On the problem of the date of carving see Brommer (1977), pp. 171–3. For the claim that the style of the frieze carries a political message see Osborne (1987), pp. 102–4.

The subject and its arrangement

For 'the locomotion of the spectator' as the source of animation see Fehl (1961), p. 9. For the argument concerning the figures standing on either side of the gods (E18–23, 43–6) see Jenkins (1985) and Nagy (1992). See also S. Woodford, 'Eponymoi or anonymoi', *Notes on the History of Art* 6, no. 4 (Summer 1987), pp. 1–5. It is uncertain to what extent the south frieze corresponds in subject matter to that on the north side. In particular, there is the question of whether there was a group of musicians on the south balancing that on the north. For a recent discussion of the problem see N. Himmelmann, 'Planung und Verdingung der Parthenon-Skulpturen', *Bathron. Beiträge zur Architektur und verwandten Künsten für Heinrich Drerup zu seinem 80. Geburtstag*, Saarbrücker Studien zur Archäologie und Alten Geschichte, Band 3 (1988), pp. 213–24.

The Panathenaic festival

For the festival and its procession see Simon (1983); Neils (1992). On the origins of the Panathenaia see J. A. Davison, 'Notes on the Panathenaea', *Journal of Hellenic Studies* 78 (1958), pp. 23–4; Robertson (1985). The procedure in the *apobates* race is described by Dionysius of Halicarnassus, *Roman Antiquities* VII, 73. The author describes races of the Roman period but explains that these are a survival of a much earlier age. Another source suggests the *apobates* leapt from the chariot and remounted it in mid-run: I. Bekker, *Anecdota Graeca*, vol. I (Berlin 1812), p. 426. For an annual *peplos* see Mansfield (1985), chapter I and *passim*.

Other interpretations

For the frieze as 'an ideal embodiment of a recurrent festival' see Robertson (1975), p. 11. For a general discussion of types of interpretation see B. S. Ridgway, *Fifth-century Styles in Greek Sculpture* (Princeton 1981), pp. 76–9. For a *mythological* interpretation see Kardara (1961). Kardara assumes that Erichthonius and Erechtheus are the same and that the names are interchangeable,

c.f. Kearns (1989), pp. 160–61: 'not always easy to distinguish'. Robertson (1985), pp. 236 and 254, thinks them to be quite distinct. In the text I have given the version of the name as it appears in the relevant ancient source. For a collection of the sources relating to Erichthonius see Powell (1906), *passim*. For another mythological interpretation see K. Jeppesen, 'Bild und Mythos an dem Parthenon', *Acta Archaeologica* 34 (1963), pp. 23–38. For the claim that the theme of the frieze is taken not from myth but from cult see Simon (1983), p. 58. For *symbolic* interpretations see R. Holloway, 'The archaic Acropolis and the Parthenon frieze', *Art Bulletin* 48 (1966), pp. 223–6; Root (1985); Castriota (1992), pp. 184–229. For a *historical* interpretation see Boardman (1977); see also id., 'The Parthenon frieze', in Berger (1984), pp. 210–15. Boardman (1977, pp. 48–9) based his count of figures on the arrangement of Schuchhardt (1930). This was in turn based upon Smith (1910), and follows Smith's mistake of illustrating forty-six instead of the correct forty-seven blocks in the south frieze. For a summary of the history of the study of the arrangement of the frieze, see pp. 49–51 below.

Time and place

For the episodic view of the frieze see Fehl (1961). For the attempt to locate the action in the *agora* see Boardman (1977 and 1984). For the idea that the central scene of the east frieze shows an examination of the *peplos* see W. Gauer, 'Was geschieht mit dem Peplos?', in Berger (1984), pp. 220–29. For the *arrephoroi* and their duties see Burkert (1966); Simon (1983), pp. 38–46. For an alternative interpretation of the votive relief from the Acropolis (2554) see O. Palagia, 'A new relief of the Graces and the Charities of Socrates', *Opes Atticae*, ed. M. Geerard *et al.* (The Hague, 1990), pp. 347–56.

Two processions?

For the idea of a secondary procession to the altar on the Acropolis see Rotroff (1977). The argument for the north and south sides of the frieze showing two separate sacrificial processions is put by Simon (1983), p. 61. Kardara (1961) also argued for two separate processions, that on the south for Ge, that on the north for Athena. See Mansfield (1985), p. 239, for the argument that Philochorus was referring to private rather than state sacrifices. For the text of Philochorus see Deubner, p. 26; Farnell (1896), vol. I, pp. 290 and 390. It should be noted that other versions of Philochorus' text give Pandora instead of Pandrosus. See 'Pandora' below.

Secret messages?

For the thought that the meaning of the frieze will remain a mystery 'until a fifth-century text is discovered which tells the truth', see Boardman (1984),

p. 215. For such a text and the notion of child-sacrifice see Connelly (1996). On the footstool in the hand of E31 see Boardman (1988), p. 10.

Numbers

For the insistence that numbers must mean something see Boardman (1984), pp. 214–15. For the four-fold division of the frieze corresponding with the four sides of the temple see Harrison (1984). For the claim that 'every figure has a name and every number bears significance' and the extreme attempt to divide the frieze into groups of ten or four see Beschi (1984), p. 181 (for the quotation) and (1985). For the eleven chariots of the north frieze see Gisler-Huwiler (1988). For the idea that the recurrence of certain numbers has to do with the planning and design of the frieze see Schuchhardt (1930), p. 277.

Chapter 3 A Poem in Stone

The frieze as symphonic poem

For Robert's musical metaphor see *Archaeologische Hermeneutik* (Berlin 1919), p. 31.

The frieze as drama

For emphasis on Greek drama as performance see O. Taplin, *Greek Tragedy in Action* (London 1978). For a playful attempt to dramatise the viewing of the Parthenon frieze through the eyes of a contemporary Athenian see Boardman (1985), pp. 40–45.

The frieze as Homeric image

For the ancient discussion of the relative merits of art and poetry see G. Watson, *Phantasia in Classical Thought* (Galway 1988), pp. 72–7. For Aristotle's distinction between poetry and history see his *Poetics*, 9.3. For the frieze as contest, pomp and sacrifice see Beschi (1984), p. 191. For the chariots of the west pediment and the idea of a race see J. Binder, 'The west pediment of the Parthenon Poseidon' in *Studies Presented to Sterling Dow* (Durham, North Carolina, 1984), pp. 15–22. For Athena as tamer of horses and inventor of the chariot see M. Detienne, 'The *Sea-Crow*' in *Myth, Religion and Society*, ed. R. L. Gordon and R. G. A. Buxton (Cambridge 1981), pp. 29–31. For Erichthonius as founder of the *apobates* race see Eratosthenes, *Catasterismi*, 13. The text is given by Powell (1906), pp. 29 and 73. For the shield of Achilles see O. Taplin, *Greece and Rome* 27 (1980), pp. 1–21.

Chapter 4 The *Peplos* Scene

Myth or cult?

For the central scene of the east frieze and a summary of interpretations see Brommer (1977), pp. 263–70. For the sex of the child E35 see Boardman (1977), p. 41; id. (1984), p. 214; id. (1988), pp. 9–10; Clairmont (1989), pp. 495–6 and Boardman's fierce reply (1991), pp. 119–21. Mansfield (1985), p. 293, follows Boardman in seeing the sex as female, identifying the child as an *arrephoros*. For a survey of various attempts at interpreting the central scene see Brommer (1977), pp. 263–70. For the relationship between the rites of the *arrephoroi* and the myth of the daughters of Kekrops see Burkert (1966). For Erysichthon as the mythical paradigm of E35 see Simon (1983), p. 67. For Pausanias' account of the myth see *Description of Greece* 1, 27, 3. For the suggestion that the stools are for Pandrosus and Ge Kourotrophos see Simon (1982), pp. 140–44; id. (1983), pp. 68–9. For sacrifices to Erechtheus/Erichthonius see Deubner, p. 27. For the stools and their many interpretations see Schäfer (1987), pp. 192 ff. (including one of his own). B. Wesenberg ('Götterfeste, Wettkämpfe und Reiterparaden' in *Blick in die Wissenschaft Forschungsmagazin der Universität Regensburg*, Heft 2, 2 (1993), pp. 32–41) has recently attempted to argue that the objects carried by figures E31 and 32 are not stools but flattish trays. He supports his interpretation by attempting to argue away the legs of the stools. He fails to explain, however, the drill holes by which the left-hand legs of both stools were attached. The right-hand leg of the stool carried by 32 is clearly shown and the right-hand leg of that carried by 31 is broken away, although a stump remains in the drapery of her left shoulder. For yet another reading of the central scene of the east frieze see H. von Heintze, 'Athena Polias am Parthenon', *Gymnasium* 100 (1993), pp. 385–418, who argues (p. 413) that the girls, 31–2, are bringing stools with folded cloths on them, these being the cult dress of the Athena Polias statue. The priest, 34, is not concerned with the new *peplos*, but is shown in the process of folding up the old cult dress (p. 410).

Rite of passage

For the importance of weaving in Greek society see I. Jenkins, 'The ambiguity of Greek textiles', *Arethusa* 18 (1985), pp. 109–28. Simon (1983), pp. 40–42, argues against Burkert, seeing the *arrephoria* as a rite of fertility rather than initiation. For A. van Gennep see *The Rites of Passage* (1908; first published in English, London 1960). It is not known at what time of the year the *arrephoroi* were elected. I have followed Simon, however, in assuming that their first duty was at the Panathenaia: Simon (1983), p. 39 (note 6) and p. 41 (note 10). For the *arrephoroi* see Mansfield (1985), chapter 5.

The peplos as emblem of cosmic order

On all aspects of the *peplos* see Mansfield (1985). See also E. Barber in Neils (1992), pp. 103–18. For a purple *peplos* woven annually see Mansfield, p. 142 and *passim*.

Pandora

For the Hesiodic myth see J.-P. Vernant, 'The myth of Prometheus in Hesiod' in *Myth, Religion and Society*, op. cit. under Chapter 3 ('The frieze as Homeric image'). For the base of the Parthenos see Leipen (1971), pp. 23–7. Boardman (1985), pp. 249–50, has looked for a more positive reading of Pandora's presence. For Robertson's view of it as a token of the 'utter unreliability of the divine' see his *A History of Greek Art* (Cambridge 1975), p. 312. For Hesiod's world view contrasted with that of Homer see J. Gould, 'On making sense of Greek religion', in *Greek Religion and Society*, ed. P. E. Easterling and J. V. Muir (Cambridge 1985), p. 25. For sacrifices to Pandora see sources collected by W. Oldfather in Pauly's *Real-Encyclopädie*, s.v. p. 530. See also Farnell (1896), p. 290. It should be noted that there is confusion between Pandora and Pandrosus in the transmission of the text of Philochorus. For Erechtheus on the base of the statue of Athena and Hephaestus see E. Harrison, 'Alkamenes' sculptures for the Hephaisteion', *American Journal of Archaeology*, three parts in vol. 81 (1977).

Bibliography

The following titles appear in abbreviated form in the Notes.

Berger (1984): E. Berger (ed.), *Parthenon-Kongress Basel, Referate und Berichte 4 bis 8 April 1982*, 2 vols (Mainz).

Berger (1988): *Kanon, Festschrift Ernst Berger*, ed. M Schmidt (Basel).

Beschi (1984): L. Beschi, 'Il fregio del Partenone: una proposta di lettura', *Atti della Accademia Nazionale dei Lincei*, pp. 173–95.

Beschi (1985): another version of Beschi (1984) in Greek, in *Archäische und Klassische Griechische Plastik*, Deutsches Archäologisches Institut Abteilung Athen, Akten des Internationalen Kolloquiums 22–25 April 1985, vol. 2 (Mainz), pp. 199–224.

Boardman (1977): J. Boardman, 'The Parthenon frieze – another view', in *Festschrift für Frank Brommer*, ed. U. Höckmann and A. Krug (Mainz), pp. 39–49.

Boardman (1984): J. Boardman, 'The Parthenon frieze', in Berger (1984), pp. 210–15.

Boardman and Finn (1985): J. Boardman and D. Finn, *The Parthenon and its Sculptures* (London).

Boardman (1988): J. Boardman, 'Notes on the Parthenon east frieze', in Berger (1988), pp. 9–14.

Boardman (1991): J. Boardman, 'The naked truth', *Oxford Journal of Archaeology* 10, 1, pp. 119–21.

Brommer (1977): F. Brommer, *Der Parthenonfries* (Mainz).

Burkert (1966): W. Burkert, 'Kekropidensage und Arrephoria', *Hermes* 94, pp. 1–25.

Castriota (1992): D. Castriota, *Myth, Ethos and Actuality, Official Art in Fifth-Century BC Athens* (Wisconsin).

Clairmont (1989): C. Clairmont, 'Girl or boy?', *Archäologischer Anzeiger*, pp. 496–7.

Connelly (1996): J. Connelly, 'Parthenon and *Parthenoi*: A Mythological Interpretation of the Parthenon Frieze', *American Journal of Archaeology* 100, pp. 58–80.

Deubner (1956): L. Deubner, *Attische Feste* (Berlin).

Dinsmoor (1954): W. Dinsmoor, 'New evidence for the Parthenon frieze', *American Journal of Archaeology* 58, pp. 144–5.

Dinsmoor (Papers): W. Dinsmoor, unpublished manuscripts held in the archives of the American School of Classical Studies, Athens.

Farnell (1896): L. R. Farnell, *The Cults of the Greek States* (Oxford).

Fehl (1961): P. Fehl, 'The rocks on the Parthenon frieze', *Journal of the Warburg and Courtauld Institutes* 24, pp. 1–44.

Gisler-Huwiler (1988): M. Gisler-Huwiler, 'A propos des apobates et de quelques cavaliers de la frise nord', in Berger (1988), pp. 15–18.

Harrison (1979): E. Harrison, Review of Brommer (1977), *American Journal of Archaeology* 83, pp. 489–91.

Harrison (1984): E. Harrison, 'Time in the Parthenon frieze', in Berger (1984), pp. 230–34.

Jenkins (1985): I. Jenkins, 'The composition of the so-called eponymous heroes on the east frieze of the Parthenon', *American Journal of Archaeology* 89, 1, pp. 121–7.

Jenkins (1990): I. Jenkins, 'Acquisition and supply of casts of the Parthenon sculptures by the British Museum 1835–1939', *Annual of the British School of Archaeology at Athens* 85, pp. 89–114.

Kardara (1961): Ch. Kardara, 'Glaukopis, the archaic naos and the theme of the Parthenon frieze', *Archaiologike Ephemeris* (1961, appeared 1964), pp. 61–158.

Kearns (1989): E. Kearns, *The Heroes of Attica, Bulletin of the Institute of Classical Studies*, Supplement 57.

Korres (1988): M. Korres, 'Überzählige Werkstücke des Parthenonfrieses', in Berger (1988), pp. 19–27.

Korres (1990): M. Korres, 'Der Parthenon bis 1687 Reparatur – Kirche – Moschee – Pulvermagazin', *Die Explosion des Parthenon* (special exhibition, Berlin, 23 June – 23 Sept.).

Bibliography

Leipen (1971): N. Leipen, *Athena Parthenos, A Reconstruction* (Toronto).

Mansfield (1985): J. Mansfield, 'The robe of Athena and the Panathenaic peplos' (PhD. dissertation, Berkeley).

Michaelis (1885): A. Michaelis, 'Die Lücken im Parthenonfries', *Archäologische Zeitung* 43, pp. 53–70.

Nagy (1992): B. Nagy, 'Athenian officials on the Parthenon frieze', *American Journal of Archaeology* 96, pp. 55–69.

Neils (1992): J. Neils (ed.), *Goddess and Polis, The Panathenaic Festival in Athens* (Princeton).

Osborne (1987): R. Osborne, 'The viewing and obscuring of the Parthenon frieze', *Journal of Hellenic Studies* 107, pp. 98–105.

Powell (1906): B. Powell, *Erichthonius and the Three Daughters of Cecrops*, Cornell Studies in Classical Philology 17 (Ithaca, N.Y.).

Robertson (1975): M. Robertson and A. Frantz, *The Parthenon Frieze* (London).

Robertson (1985): N. Robertson, 'The origin of the Panathenaea', *Rheinisches Museum für Philologie* 128, pp. 231–95.

Root (1985): M. C. Root, 'The Parthenon frieze and the Apadana reliefs at Persepolis', *American Journal of Archaeology* 89, pp. 103–20.

Rotroff (1977): S. Rotroff, 'The Parthenon frieze and the sacrifice to Athena', *American Journal of Archaeology* 81, pp. 379–82.

Schäfer (1987): T. Schäfer, 'Diphroi und Peplos auf dem Ostfries des Parthenon', *Mitteilungen des Deutschen Archäologischen Instituts, Athenische Abteilung* 102, pp. 85–122.

Schuchhardt (1930): W.-H. Schuchhardt, 'Die Entstehung des Parthenonfrieses', *Jahrbuch des Deutschen Archäologischen Instituts* 45, pp. 218–80.

Simon (1982): E. Simon, 'Die Mittelszene im Ostfries des Parthenon', *Mitteilungen des Deutschen Archäologischen Instituts, Athenische Abteilung* 97, pp. 127–44.

Simon (1983): E. Simon, *Festivals of Attica* (Wisconsin).

Smith (1910): A. H. Smith, *The Sculptures of the Parthenon* (London).

Wycherley (1978): R. E. Wycherley, *The Stones of Athens* (Princeton).

The Arrangement of the Frieze

The arrangement of the frieze illustrated here draws on the efforts of successive generations of scholars who have endeavoured to reassemble the scattered remains of the Parthenon sculptures. The photographs are those prepared originally by Frederick Anderson for A. H. Smith's monumental *The Sculptures of the Parthenon* (1910), the last attempt by the British Museum to publish a complete record of the Parthenon frieze using both original sculpture and reproductions in plaster cast. Smith's handsome photogravure plates have been edited and rearranged to take account of more recent thinking on the original sequence of the sculptures.

Of an original 524 feet (160 m), a total of some 420 feet (128 m) of the frieze has survived. Of this, around sixty per cent is in the British Museum, having been removed from the Acropolis at the beginning of the nineteenth century by the agents of Lord Elgin. The remainder is largely in Athens or dispersed among a number of European collections, including those of Paris, Rome, Palermo, Vienna and Heidelberg. After the Greek War of Independence (1821–32) a great many sculptures were disinterred on the Acropolis. These had been buried or incorporated into buildings, and were therefore overlooked by Elgin's men. Other pieces had already been taken away by travellers who visited the Acropolis before Elgin, and were subsequently rediscovered in European collections. In several instances the British Museum actually acquired the original fragment, but more usually, as in the case of the finds made on the Acropolis after independence, a plaster cast was commissioned and this was fitted to the frieze displayed in the British Museum. By this means an understanding of the arrangement of the frieze on the building was built up. The Museum steadily increased its collection of casts, and by taking new moulds from these and from the original sculptures it supplied numerous copies on demand to museums, universities and other institutions, both public and private, all over Britain, Europe and America. Thus the body of knowledge accumulated in the Elgin Room of the British Museum in the nineteenth century was circulated abroad (Jenkins 1990).

It is some fifty years since the Museum displayed casts of the Parthenon frieze with original sculpture in the same gallery. The information that these casts provide is now largely published and the originals are shown free of cast copies. The casts are nonetheless carefully preserved as a research resource, and in some instances they serve in place of pieces that were discovered on the Acropolis after the War of Independence but which have since disappeared. The earliest casts acquired by the Museum, not only of the Parthenon sculpture but also of other monuments in Athens, were supplied by Lord Elgin himself. The west side of the Parthenon was least affected by the explosion of 1687, and here the frieze and its supporting architecture were still largely in place when he visited the Acropolis at the beginning of the nineteenth century. Elgin's men removed only the corner block of the west frieze, where it ran onto the north side, and the block immediately adjacent to it. From the remainder they took negative moulds and these were used to make positive casts. Now, after some 200 years, these casts give a fuller record of the original sculpture than the sculpture itself. Already by the time a second set of moulds was taken from it, around 1870, the west frieze had suffered serious depredation from the weather (Jenkins 1990). In 1993 it was removed from the building and after conservation is destined for the shelter of a museum.

The German scholar Adolph Michaelis was the first to attempt a comprehensive publication of the frieze in a study making full use of the casts assembled in the British Museum (published in 1871). It had been preceded in the Museum by a number of lesser works, including the volumes devoted to the Parthenon sculptures in the series *Museum Marbles*, and afterwards by a succession of Museum Guides. In 1910 Michaelis' account was itself superseded by the British Museum's own publication, the fruit of many years' labour by A. H. Smith. His arrangement of the frieze has since been revised in the light of more recent studies. This process of revision had already begun in 1928 in the sixth edition of the *Guide to the Department of Greek and Roman Antiquities*. Further adjustments were made in the arrangement of the frieze in the Museum gallery itself when in 1949 the sculpture was brought out of wartime storage and redisplayed by Bernard Ashmole, then Keeper of Greek and Roman Antiquities. Some of these improvements were incorporated into the arrangement proposed by William B. Dinsmoor Sr, who made considerable advances in our understanding of the number and sequence of the original frieze blocks (Dinsmoor 1954 and Papers). As a trained architect, Dinsmoor was able to take into account the evidence of both sculpture and architecture, that is to say architrave blocks that were originally placed below the frieze, and cornice blocks above it. In addition, Dinsmoor's interest in the problem was assisted by Benjamin D. Meritt's discovery in 1946, in the library of the Royal Society in London, of an important manuscript by Francis Vernon, who had described the Parthenon as it appeared in 1675, only twelve years before the explosion that was to wreck the building. The Vernon manuscript is of especial importance in indicating the presence of six hitherto unknown windows (three on each of the long flanks) cut through the frieze to light the interior of the temple at some date during its later history as a church. This new evidence was combined with the drawings by the Flemish artist Jacques Carrey, who in 1674 had made a valuable record of many of the Parthenon sculptures. These have long served archaeologists as evidence for reconstructing the appearance of sculptures destroyed or dislodged by the explosion. Before the discovery of the Vernon manuscript, however, proper attention had not been given to the indications in Carrey's drawings of windows in the frieze. By correlating the explicit evidence of the Vernon manuscript with the hitherto obscure 'window' annotations in Carrey's drawings, Dinsmoor was able to make better sense of the drawings as a basis for reconstructing the original sequence of the frieze.

Dinsmoor unfortunately never published in full his reordering of the frieze blocks and there followed two imperfect attempts to illustrate the whole length of the frieze. The first, by Martin Robertson and Alison Frantz (1975), avoids all discussion of the problems of arrangement, while the second, by Frank Brommer (1977), considers them but comes to some unsatisfactory conclusions. A valuable review of the latter by Professor Evelyn Harrison (1979) sets out the principal objections. Meanwhile, in the Basel Skulpturhalle, a cast reconstruction of the frieze, conceived by Ernst Berger, has recently been completed with the help of Madeleine Gisler-Huwiler. The Basel arrangement follows closely that suggested by Dinsmoor and has the advantage of trying the proposed placement of blocks and fragments in portable cast form on a mock-up of the Parthenon's entablature. The Basel experiment is a remarkable achievement and represents a considerable advance in the search for a definitive solution to the problem of arrangement. There is still, however, room for dissent and the sequence set out here, while owing much to the reasoning of the Dinsmoor–Basel arrangement, nevertheless offers an alternative based upon the author's own observations.

One major difference between the Dinsmoor arrangement and my own concerns the last eight blocks of the south frieze at the east end, showing cattle as victims. Since 1954, when Dinsmoor published a brief note of his revised sequence, scholars have followed him almost without exception. Brommer (1977, pl. 113) illustrated Dinsmoor's arrangement of the victims of the south frieze and was followed by Beschi (1984 and 1985) and again by Boardman (1985, p. 243). Harrison (1979 and 1982) also accepted the Dinsmoor sequence. My own arrangement does not follow Dinsmoor but maintains the sequence of blocks first proposed by Michaelis (1885) and which still persists in the exhibition at the British Museum. The arguments in favour of preferring Michaelis' arrangement over Dinsmoor's are complex and are to be published separately in a forthcoming article. Suffice it here to say that, by combining Michaelis' arrangement with the best of Dinsmoor's, it has been possible to propose a sequence of figures in the south frieze which corresponds more closely than thought previously with that of the north frieze. Thus the frieze is here reconstructed to include, ahead of the chariots, elders, musicians, *hydriaphoroi* and tray-bearers on both the long north and south sides.

Numbering of frieze blocks and individual figures

This book has taken the momentous step of giving a new running sequence of numbers to the individual blocks of the frieze and a separate sequence to the human figures carved on them. The conventional system of numbering goes back to Michaelis' publication of 1871. In the course of repeated revisions his original sequence has become confused and confusing to scholar and student alike. For the sake of clarity, therefore, it has been decided to create a new sequence of numbers which will henceforth be adopted both in the British Museum's official publications and in its public exhibition of the sculptures themselves.

(*Right*) Concordance of the arrangement of frieze blocks as numbered in this book (**in bold type**) and the Michaelis/Dinsmoor numbering. The numbering of the east and west friezes remains unchanged.

SOUTH FRIEZE		NORTH FRIEZE	
WEST TO EAST			
I	I	**XLVII**	XLII
II	II	**XLVI**	XLI
III	III	**XLV**	XL
IV	IV	**XLIV**	XXXIX
V	V	**XLIII**	XXXVIII
VI	VI	**XLII**	XXXVII
VII	VII	**XLI**	XXXVI
VIII	VIII	**XL**	XXXV
IX	IX	**XXXIX**	XXXIV
X	X	**XXXVIII**	XXXIII
XI	XI	**XXXVII**	XXXII
XII	XII	**XXXVI**	XXXI
XIII	XIII	**XXXV**	XXX
XIV	XIV	**XXXIV**	XXIX
XV	XV	**XXXIII**	XXVIII
XVI	XVI	**XXXII**	XXVII
XVII	XVII	**XXXI**	XXVI
XVIII	XVIII	**XXX**	XXV
XIX	XIX	**XXIX**	XXIV
XX	XX	**XXVIII**	XXIII
XXI	XXI	**XXVII**	XXII
XXII	XXI★	**XXVI**	XXI
XXIII	XXII	**XXV**	XX
XXIV	XXIII	**XXIV**	XVIII
XXV	XXIV	**XXIII**	XVII
XXVI	XXV	**XXII**	XIX★★★
XXVII	XXVI	**XXI**	XIX★★
XXVIII	XXVII	**XX**	XIX★
XXIX	XXIX	**XIX**	XIX
XXX	XXIX★	**XVIII**	XVI★
XXXI	XXX	**XVII**	XVI
XXXII	XXXI	**XVI**	XV
XXXIII	XXXII	**XV**	XIV
XXXIV	XXXIII	**XIV**	XIII★
XXXV	XXXIV	**XIII**	XIII
XXXVI	XXXV	**XII**	XII
XXXVII	XXXVI	**XI**	XI
XXXVIII	XXXVI★	**X**	X
XXXIX	XXXVII	**IX**	IX
XL	XXXVII★	**VIII**	VIII
XLI	XLI	**VII**	VII
XLII	XLIII(a)	**VI**	VI
XLIII	XXXIX	**V**	V
XLIV	XL	**IV**	IV
XLV	XLII	**III**	III
XLVI	XXXVIII	**II**	II
XLVII	XLIV + XLIII(b)	**I**	I

Fragments of the frieze

Since A. H. Smith published his book in 1910, from which the photographs in this publication are largely taken, numerous additional fragments of sculpture have been assigned to the frieze, while others known to him have been reassigned. A full documentary history of the study of the arrangement of the frieze will soon be published by Ernst Berger and Madeleine Gisler-Huwiler based upon the Basel reconstruction of the frieze in cast form. Meanwhile, I have drawn upon the following publications for information and illustrations regarding the principal fragments unknown to Smith: M. Bruskari, *Athenische Mitteilungen* 75 (1960), pp. 4–8; Brommer (1977), pp. 125–42; G. Despinis, *Parthenonia* (Athens 1982), pp. 1–14; A. Mantis, *Archäische und Klassische Griechische Plastik, Akten des Internationalen Kolloquiums 22–25 April 1985 in Athen*, vol. 2 (Mainz 1985), p. 75.

Drawings of the frieze

Photographs of actual sculpture are here supplemented with drawings of missing parts. Drawn by Sue Bird, these are based in most places upon the drawings of the frieze attributed to the Flemish artist Jacques Carrey, thought to have been made in 1674 for the Marquis de Nointel. Carrey's drawings, however, do not exist for all missing sculpture, nor can they be relied upon for accuracy in every situation. There is, therefore, scope for conjecture and for improvement over Carrey. It is known, for example, that where Carrey drew two horses per chariot, there were in fact four. Again, on the south frieze Carrey drew figures (s107–10) carrying oblong-shaped objects which some have interpreted as inscribed tablets (*pinakes*). Little survives of this group, but from the physical remains of one figure and from a comparison with a group of figures on the north frieze it is clear that what Carrey saw were not *pinakes* but the broken remains of the sounding box of a musical instrument called a kithara. In such cases Carrey's drawings have been edited to take account of improvements based upon archaeological knowledge.

(*Overleaf*) Chariot group (south frieze XXXI, British Museum).

The South Frieze

Athens   London   Athens

The procession of the south frieze runs parallel with that on the north side
of the building and has the same directional flow, from west to east.
Beginning at the south-west corner, it occupies the whole of the south side,
before turning the corner onto the east. The southern branch of the
procession follows a similar, although not identical pattern to the northern.
It begins with mounted horsemen, and ahead of them come chariots.
Further ahead still come groups of pedestrian figures: bringing up the rear
of these are a group of elders; they are preceded by musicians and others
carrying trays of offerings, and ahead of them men leading cattle for sacrifice.

The South Frieze

don   Athens   (London)   London

Rounding the eastern corner we find girls led by a marshal towards standing dignitaries and, finally, the gods.

The horsemen of the south frieze are less well preserved than those of the north, and the composition is less varied. A total of sixty riders is divided into ten ranks, each group being shown with its own particular dress. This grouping may reflect the ten-fold tribal division of the Athenian cavalry. The first figure of the south frieze is a marshal facing towards the east. On the same weathered block are shown three of a group of six horsemen (s2–7) wearing a short cloak (*chlamys*), tunic, knee-length boots and a type of cap with ear- and neck-flaps, commonly worn in ancient Thrace. Ahead, the dress of the second rank of riders (s8–13) is less certain but appears to be a *chlamys* worn without tunic, hat or boots. The cloak of s8 has blown back from the body, and his nudity punctuates the division between the first and second ranks of riders. The leading horseman of the second rank (s13) turns round to check on the progress of his companions, and this action serves equally to mark the division of the second and third ranks. The flickering manes of the horses are a feature of the second rank, and all six riders may have been carved by the same hand.

London   London

The South Frieze

don   London

The third rank of riders (s14–19) is arranged as before, horses overlapping one another. They go bareheaded, and their dress is a short tunic with boots. The riders of the fourth group (s20–25) wear a *chlamys* draped over a tunic, but neither hat nor boots. All the horsemen of the cavalcade are disproportionately large in comparison with their mounts, and the human subject is thereby given greater prominence. This is partly achieved by the fact that, while the foreparts of the horse are usually rearing off the ground, the hind legs are flexed, reducing the overall height of the horse and thus creating more space for the human figure. Rather than seeing the horses at full gallop, therefore, we seem to see them reined in at the end of a run. Indeed, the overall mood of both the horse and chariot parades is one of restrained energy.

London   London   (face of 30 Athens)

The South Frieze

don   London   Athens

An intentional gap in the composition marks the division between the fourth and fifth groups of riders (s20–25, 26–31). The distinction between the fifth group and the sixth (s32–7) – in so far as the damaged state allows us to see it – is emphasised by a compositional break in the pattern of overlapping. The fifth group (26–31) is distinctively dressed in body armour worn over a short tunic. The armour is made out of two parts hinged at the sides, beaten to the shape of a male torso. Boots are worn, but no hats. The sixth group (32–7) also wears armour, but of a different kind. This is made of plates of reinforced leather, comprising a corslet, shoulder straps and waistband hung with a series of straps or *pteryges*. The riders wear boots and a cap with a long tail.

All the horsemen of the frieze are shown without stirrups, which were not invented before the medieval period, and no saddles are indicated. It is possible that during a parade the Athenian cavalry rode bareback, but it could not dispense with reins or bridle. Holes in appropriate places indicate where these were once added to the frieze in metal.

59

Athens   London   Athens and conjectured

The South Frieze

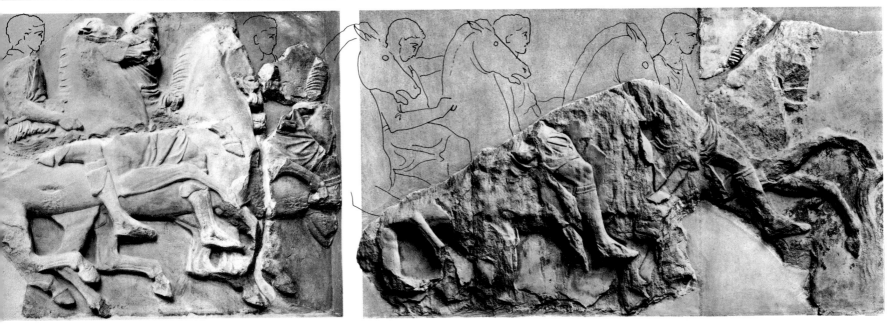

Athens and conjectured

(Athens) London

Again a short break in the rhythm of the riders serves to punctuate the division between the sixth and seventh ranks. The horse of the hindmost rider of group seven (s38–43) rears at a steeper angle than his near neighbours. The seventh group wears a helmet of the Athenian type, which is open-faced, unlike the Corinthian form with its nose-piece and cheek protection.

In addition we can make out a *chlamys*, tunic and boots. Of the eighth rank (s44–9) at least the hindmost rider (s44) wears the pelt of some animal over his tunic. The stiff leathery skin can be seen streaming behind into the space separating his rank from the preceding one. The eighth group also wears boots.

Athens and Carrey   London   (Athens)   conjectured

The South Frieze

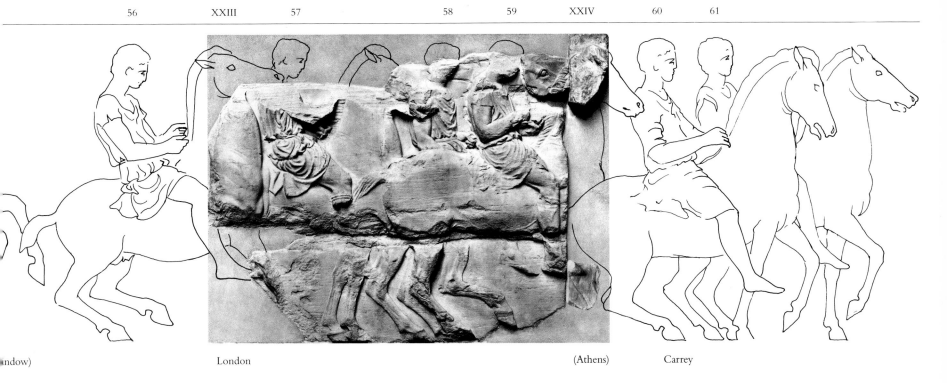

ndow)   London   (Athens)   Carrey

The leading horse of the eighth group (s49) rears sharply into the open space separating his rank from the hindmost mount of the ninth (s50–55). This group wears a *chlamys* over a short tunic and boots. Most noticeable is the broad-brimmed all-weather hat (*petasos*). The division between the ninth and the tenth rank of riders has been obscured by the cutting of a window into the frieze during the Middle Ages. The syntax of the composition can, however, be reconstructed with a pause between the two ranks. The regular overlapping rhythm of the south cavalcade is broken in the tenth rank as the horsemen gather into an irregular bunch. The foremost pair of horses seem to stand still, except for one hoof raised in anticipation. The uniform of the tenth group is a tunic and boots.

London and Carrey   (Athens)   (Athens)   London and Carrey

The South Frieze

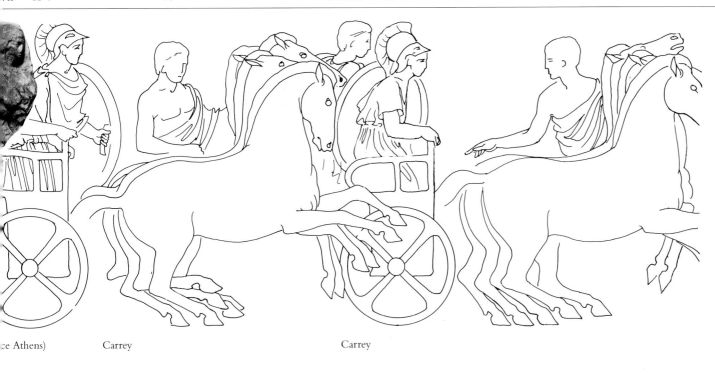

The cavalcade comes to rest behind the chariots, and the first of the ten chariots is also stationary. This block has suffered much damage, but on the left it is still possible to make out the round shield of a foot soldier (s63). Another such figure is better seen on the next block (XXVI). Here s66, standing with all his weight on the left leg, supports a shield on his left arm. He is dressed in a tunic hitched up at the waist and a cloak falling from his shoulder. The wheel of the chariot is shown beyond the legs of s66, and behind his left shoulder can be seen the long flowing drapery of a charioteer, who has mounted the car. A marshal, s67, his right arm raised, is shown on the far side of the horses. In the next two blocks (XXVII–XXVIII) both foot soldier and charioteer have mounted the chariot.

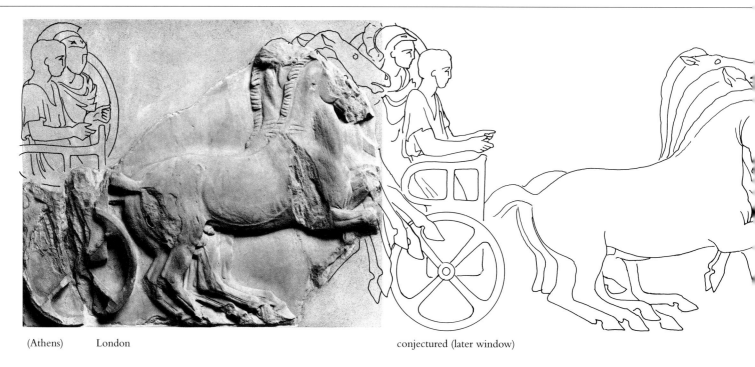

(Athens)   London   conjectured (later window)

The South Frieze

lon   London and Carrey

The explosion of 1687 tore out the long sides of the Parthenon, and the middle section of the frieze took the full impact of the blast. This accounts for the broken state of the chariot blocks today. Even before the explosion, a window cut into the frieze destroyed the sixth chariot. Fortunately, the beautiful seventh chariot group (XXXI) is preserved. Here in shallow relief is carved a team of four horses. The flickering manes of their tossing necks remind us of those already noticed in the second rank of mounted horsemen.

The motif is picked up in the fiery crest of the helmet of the foot soldier s79 riding in the chariot and again in the wind-blown folds of his flying cloak. The charioteer, partially visible on the extreme left of the slab, is arched back in the car, using his body as a counter-weight to the forward thrust of the horses. He reins them to a skidding halt; the reins were once added in metal and are now lost.

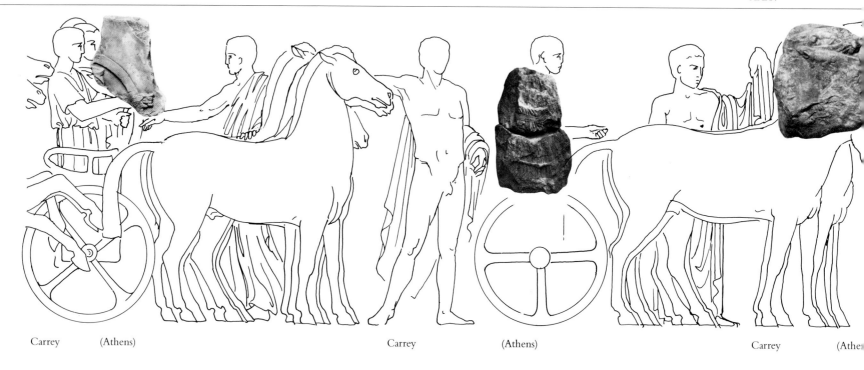

Carrey   (Athens)   Carrey   (Athens)   Carrey   (Athens)

The South Frieze

London and Carrey   Athens/Carrey and conjectured

Carrey's drawings enable us to see how, ahead of the dramatic block XXXI, the chariots are brought to rest in anticipation of the groups of figures who walk in front (89–106). These are often identified with the *thallophoroi* or branch-bearers, men who – having been judged the most handsome in a Panathenaic beauty contest – then walked in the procession carrying the victor's olive branch. There is, however, no trace of a branch, and although it has been suggested that these were painted onto the stone, some other identification seems more probable. There were a number of officials involved in the organisation of the games and the sacrifices, and they may be represented here. These men are led by a further four figures (107–10) whom Carrey drew bearing flat board-like objects. A part only of one of

these is preserved on the extreme right of the much-damaged block XXXVII (S107).

The identification of these objects is disputed and the interpretation preferred here, doubting the accuracy of Carrey's drawing, sees them as representing the sounding box of a stringed musical instrument, a kithara. The intricate superstructure of the instrument is assumed to have broken away already by Carrey's time. The restored drawing shows a group of four musicians, balancing those of the north frieze. In support of this interpretation it has been observed that figure S107 holds an object in his broken right hand which may plausibly be seen as a plectrum.

Carrey and conjectured (later window)   conjectured   conjectured   (Athens)

The South Frieze

London   Athens and conjectured

A window later cut into the frieze destroyed the sequence of figures immediately ahead of figure S107. In addition to the kitharists a group of pipe-players is restored here, balancing those on the north frieze and, ahead of them, four figures carrying water-jars (S115–18). These vessels probably held the water which was a necessary accompaniment to the purification rites attending the meat sacrifice. A fragment is assigned to the next block, which is largely missing. This shows part of the figure of a youth (S120) carrying something upon his shoulder. This was a shallow boat-shaped

vessel similar to that borne by three figures shown together on the north frieze (N13–15). From literary sources we learn that metics, the non-citizen workers resident in the city, carried such a container in the Panathenaic procession, filled with honeycombs and small cakes. The Greek word is *skaphe*, from which we derive our 'skiff'. As on the north frieze, the *skaphephoroi* walk immediately behind the sacrificial victims, and the trays perhaps contain the cakes placed upon the sacrificial altar with the intention of luring the cattle to it.

London   London   London

The South Frieze

London and conjectured

This is one of the most beautiful passages of the entire frieze, showing cattle being led as sacrificial victims. The sequence of blocks is uncertain, but that followed here seems likely on compositional grounds. The procession of victims has begun quietly enough, but the beast shown on block XLIII is exhibiting signs of distress and has to be restrained. A youth (S130) wedges his foot against a rock and strains on the halter, which was added in metal and is now lost. The disturbance has a knock-on effect and another youth (S133) looks round to observe the commotion behind him. At the same time he shortens the tether of the beast under his charge. A second youth (S135) reaches out to assist him and also looks back. Meanwhile the animal registers a protest by straining its neck upwards, and this pathetic image is thought to have inspired Keats to write of the 'heifer lowing at the skies'. The tilt of the nose of this beast breaks through the line formed by the backs of the other cattle, as they follow one another. This line is level at first, but is then distorted into a rising wave by the excitement of the animal managed by S130. It dips before rising to a peak with the nose of Keats' heifer, and then falls once more, until it is brought level again towards the end of the sequence. Thus we can follow the mood of the victims from quiet resignation, through varying degrees of disquiet, until calm is restored.

The design and carving of the cattle is a *tour de force*, and particularly pleasing is the subtle modelling of the broad flanks of the beasts, contrasting with the drapery of the youths who lead them.

London and conjectured   London

The South Frieze

The East Frieze

I   1   II   2   3   4   5   6   III   7   8   9   10   11

(Athens)   London   (Athens)   (London)   Carrey   Athens and Carrey   (Athens)   London

The East Frieze

76

(Athens)   London

Turning the corner from the south onto the east frieze we first meet a marshal (E1), placed there as if to beckon us to follow him. The gesture of his raised right hand and crooked finger is, in fact, directed at the procession of the south frieze. He looks back over his shoulder and his right foot trails back to fill the angle of the corner, but the strong *contrapposto* of his body inclines towards the scene ahead. There we suddenly find, for the first time on the frieze, a solemn procession of girls, heavily draped in mantle and tunic. The first five carry shallow bowls (*phialai*) to be used in the pouring of ritual libations, and the next five are shown with jugs. Ahead of these, two pairs of girls (E12–15) each carry a peculiar trumpet-shaped object, usually seen as a stand for burning incense, comparable with that carried by figure 57 further ahead on the east frieze. These are shorter in length, however, and the upper end is drilled for some attachment. We may perhaps

see here the stands for supporting the spit on which the meat was roasted. The foremost pair of girls stand quietly waiting, empty-handed.

At the head of the procession there stands a group of men (E18–23) draped in simple cloaks (*himation*). Some scholars read them as three pairs of non-processional figures and, taking them together with four similar (E43–6) on the north side of the gods, see them as the ten eponymous heroes of Athens. Others would take figure E18 as a marshal and link him directly with the head of the cortège. This then leaves nine figures, all distinguished by their staves. Figure E19 is one of the nine, but is shown in conversation with the marshal E18. He and his neighbours cannot, therefore, be regarded as being above mortal status and, on this reading, figures E19–23 (and 43–6) are seen as civic dignitaries, possibly magistrates waiting to preside over the ceremonies.

77

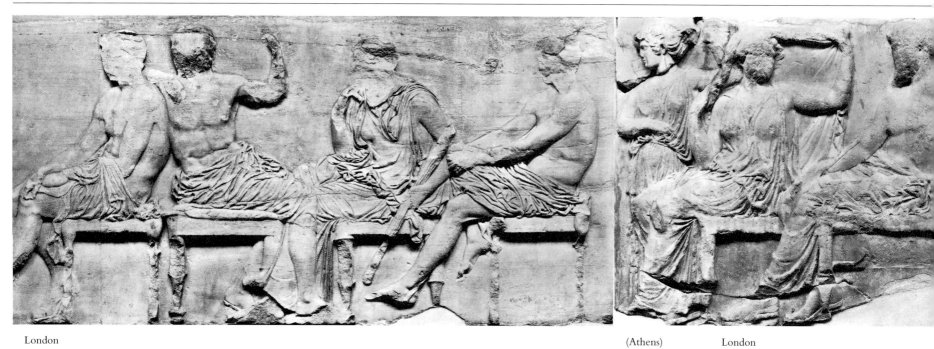

London   (Athens)   London

At the centre of the east frieze the gods are shown seated waiting for the ceremonies to begin. They are divided into two groups, one (E24–30) facing the southern branch of the procession, while the other (E36–42) looks to the north. On the extreme left Hermes is shown with a hat (*petasos*) resting on his knee. Being the messenger god, he needs this to protect his head from sun and rain when going about his business. On his feet he wears short boots (possibly winged), and a drill-hole in the right hand indicates that he was holding his wand (*caduceus*). Next to Hermes another male figure twists round in his seat to observe the approaching procession. One arm rests on the shoulder of his companion, while the other is supported by a staff (now lost). He is thought to be Dionysus, god of wine, and the staff must therefore have been a rod crowned with a pine cone, as seen in numerous representations on painted vases. Dionysus' right leg overlaps with the left foot of the next figure (E26), whose cult was closely linked with his own. This is Demeter,

goddess of growing grain. She sits with her head resting on one hand, and in the other she carries a torch of tightly bound straw. Her somewhat melancholy manner is intentional: the myth of her cult (centred on the mysteries at Eleusis) was the loss of her daughter Persephone to Hades, god of the Underworld. Demeter's grief cast the world into perpetual winter, relieved only when her daughter was returned to her for a period each year, thus heralding the arrival of every new spring.

Seated next to Demeter is Ares, god of war. He cradles one knee in his clasped hands, while the other leg rests on a spear, part of which is preserved beneath the left ankle. The rest must have been painted in. Standing next to him, but more closely linked with Hera immediately to her left, is Iris, the female messenger of the gods (E28). The gesture of her raised left hand echoes that of Hera and Dionysus, although in this case the motive is quite different: Dionysus' is one of indolent support, while Hera, as goddess of

Ion

marriage, makes the bridal gesture of holding out her veil. Iris, meanwhile, arranges her hair, which we can imagine tangled by the wind while in performance of some errand. By the side of Hera, Zeus (E30) leans over the back of a throne. In his right hand he holds a sceptre. As father of the gods, his seat is distinguished from those of the other gods, who occupy simple stools. The arm-rest is supported by a miniature sphinx.

Between the two ranks of seated gods a group of figures are involved in a ritual which has to do with the piece of cloth held up by a man and a child (E34–5). This is thought to be the *peplos* or robe of Athena, woven anew every four years and dedicated on the occasion of the Great Panathenaic festival. The man wears the long ungirt tunic of a priest and is usually identified with the *archon basileus*, the chief magistrate and overseer of Athenian state religion. The child is probably a boy and may be identified as a temple-server like the boy Ion in the play of that name by Euripides.

The woman with her back to the priest is likely to be the priestess of Athena Polias. She is about to receive the cushioned stool carried by the girl approaching her. Another girl (E31) approaches behind the first, carrying both a stool and, on her left arm, a footstool. This last is much damaged but the unmistakable paw-shaped foot of one leg is preserved. The entire group of figures was carved, together with the pair of gods to left and right, on a long block placed immediately over the doorway giving access to the interior of the temple and the statue of Athena. On the extreme right of the block, Athena is shown seated with Hephaestus (E36–7). In her lap can be seen the snake fringe of the *aegis*, which the goddess wore for protection. Drill-holes on her right side indicate the line of her spear. Hephaestus, being the smith of the gods, is heavily muscled but supports his right side with a crutch under the arm. This is a reminder of the god's lameness, occasioned by his fall when hurled out of heaven by Zeus, only later to be reinstated.

Athens   (Athens)   (Palermo)   casts in Paris   (London)

The East Frieze

Next to Hephaestus comes Poseidon, god of the sea (E38). He looks straight ahead in the direction of the oncoming procession and taps his companion Apollo on the shoulder, as if to warn him of its imminent arrival. The youthful god turns around in response to his companion's signal. Beside him his sister Artemis, the huntress, adjusts her dress with one hand, while linking the other through the right arm of Aphrodite (E41). The arm movements of Poseidon, Apollo and Artemis create a pleasing sequence, culminating in the pointing gesture of the love-goddess Aphrodite who, of all the gods, makes the most explicit acknowledgment of the procession. She is accompanied by her son Eros, who holds a parasol to shade his tender skin from the scorching sun.

Next to the gods on the north side of the east frieze, balancing the standing male figures to the south, comes a group of four men (E43–6) each leaning on a stick and seemingly engaged in conversation. These are seen

London   Paris

either as magistrates or four of the ten eponymous heroes who gave their names to the ten tribes of Athens. Whatever their identity, their role in the composition is clear, namely to make a transition between the gods seated on one side and the procession approaching on the other. Lounging on staves, they are pictorially half-way between the seated gods and the fully upright processional figures.

Immediately on the right of them two marshals stand back to back. One E48) gazes towards the procession, while the other turns his back and beckons with his raised right arm and crooked finger. His gesture must be intended for the head of the procession on the south side of the east frieze. Here we have a subtle reminder that the two processions are in fact one. Figures E47 and 48 are counterpoints of each other: the one static, the other dynamic; one perpendicular, the other bent like a bow; one intent on the procession of the north side, the other occupied with that on the south.

Together, they act as a pivot on which the action of the frieze turns from the procession proper to the figures waiting at the head of it, first the standing magistrates or heroes lounging on staves and then the seated gods.

On the right of these two, another marshal (E49) is shown receiving an offering basket from one of the pair of girls facing him. Yet another marshal (E52) stands facing another pair of girls, who wait empty-handed. A drill-hole near his right hand indicates that he held something added in metal. A further pair of girls follow, one looking back to check on the progress of the procession coming up from behind. The drapery folds of the figures in this block appear sharper than those of the figures who follow to the right. The reason is the recutting of the stone as part of a restoration in the early nineteenth century.

London   (heads in Athens)   Stuart   (Athens)

Approaching the northern limit of the east frieze, we meet girls walking in single file, the delicate folds of their drapery falling, in the instance of E58 and 59, like the fluting of an architectural column. In this respect they call to mind the Caryatids who, substituting for columns, supported the south-west porch of the Ionic temple on the north side of the Acropolis known as the Erechtheum. The foremost of the girls on the Parthenon frieze carries a tall object on a flaring base, a stand (*thymiaterion*) for burning incense. From the perforated cone at the top, the sweet-smelling smoke would have drifted out over the sacrificial proceedings.

The North Frieze

Carrey   (Athens)   (Athens)   Athens   (Athe

The North Frieze

rey   Athens and Carrey   Athens and Carrey   London   Carrey

The north frieze follows a similar, if not identical, pattern to that of the south. Reading it from east to west, it will be viewed in reverse order from that of the southerly procession. At the north-east corner a youth stands facing the foremost victim, which has reached a momentary pause in the progression to the altar. The animal immediately behind seems also to have come to a standstill and waits patiently, unaffected by the apparent excitement of the third victim, who bucks violently with both fore legs off the ground. Another, quieter beast follows and behind him a group of four sheep. The transition between the victims and the next group is marked by a marshal (N12), who turns to look back and so into the face of the foremost of three tray-bearers (N13–15). A possible clue to their identity is given by the lexicographers of late antiquity, who speak of metics – non-citizen workers resident in Athens – carrying metal trays filled with honeycombs and cakes.

85

Rome   Athens   (Athens)   Carrey   (Athens)

The North Frieze

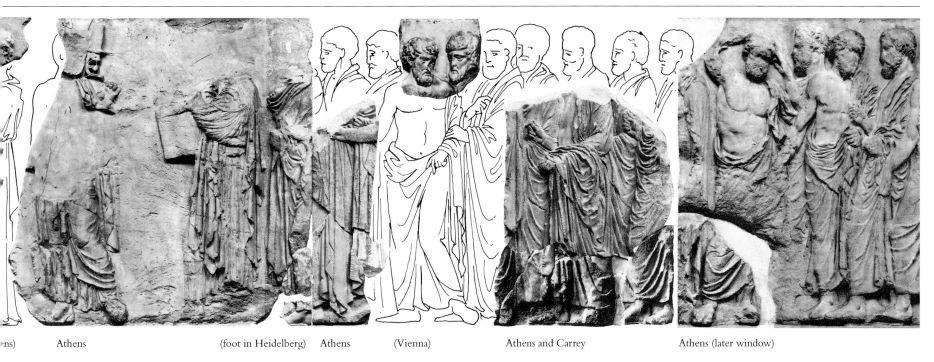

ns)   Athens   (foot in Heidelberg) Athens   (Vienna)   Athens and Carrey   Athens (later window)

The tray-bearers are followed by four youths with water-jars. Three have them on their shoulders, while a fourth is shown raising his from the ground. Four pipe-players follow, and behind these come four more musicians, heavily draped in mantle and long tunic, and carrying the large

stringed instrument known as a kithara. Behind them a group of sixteen elders (N28–43), balancing those to the south, forms a crowd advancing ahead of the chariots. The hindmost figure looks back nervously over his shoulder as a chariot skids to a halt immediately behind.

Athens and Carrey   London and Carrey   (Athens)   (Athens)

The North Frieze

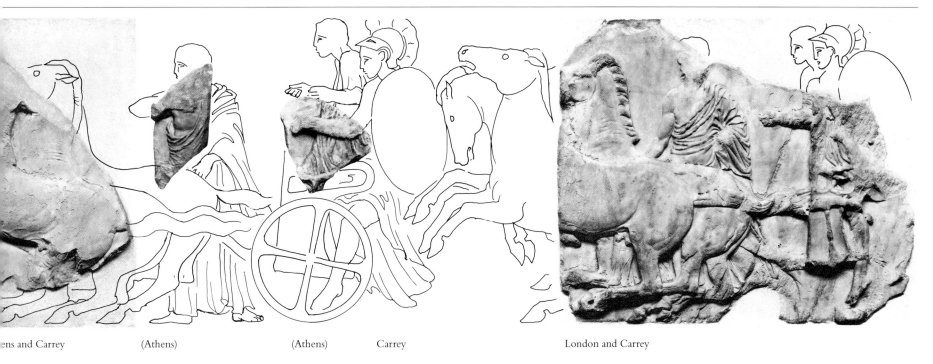

ens and Carrey   (Athens)   (Athens)   Carrey   London and Carrey

The message of blocks XI–XII of the north frieze is unequivocal: the chariot charge must be seen to come to a halt so as not to appear to run into the back of the elders walking ahead. An athletic marshal (N44) thrusts himself between the pedestrian group and the leading chariot. The chariot team rears over him as it is brought up sharply by the action of the driver (N46). He is shown bent at the waist and leaning back, far out of the carriage, thus creating a counter-balance to the forward motion of the horses. At the same time he pulls back on the reins, which were attached in metal and linked to the horses' heads. In order to emphasise the sensation of arrested energy,

a marshal turns swiftly to face the chariot behind and raises his right arm, signalling it to stop. At the same time a foot soldier (N47) in full armour has leapt out of the leading chariot and looks back, with shield arm raised, as he checks his pace to avoid the traffic.

The chariot team immediately behind is reined in accordingly, and the horses' hooves plough the air as their foreparts leave the ground. Another soldier (N50) drops one leg to the earth and prepares to slip from the carriage and join the race to the finishing post on foot, while a similar picture is developing behind.

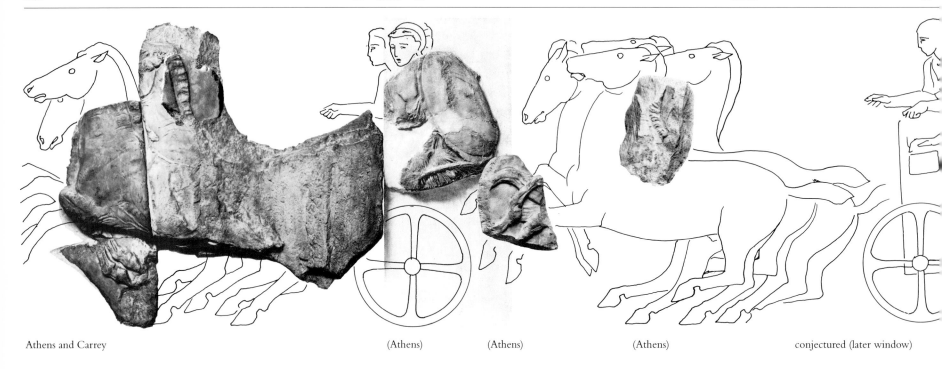

Athens and Carrey   (Athens)   (Athens)   (Athens)   conjectured (later window)

The North Frieze

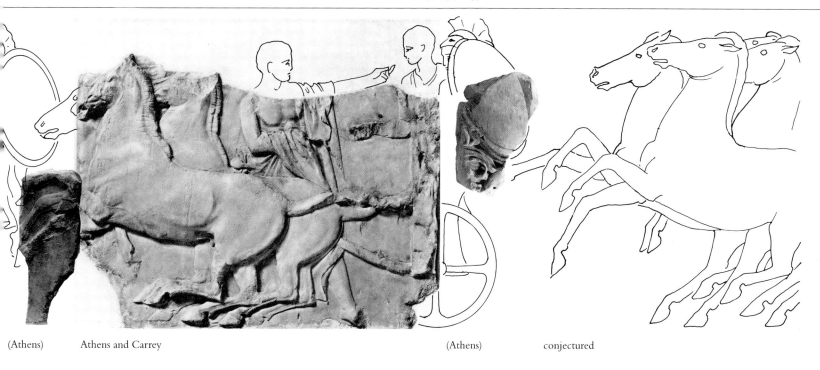

(Athens) Athens and Carrey (Athens) conjectured

The chariot sequence of the north frieze is very fragmentary and much of
it must be restored with the help of Carrey's drawings. A window cut
through the frieze in late antiquity matches that in the same position on the
south.

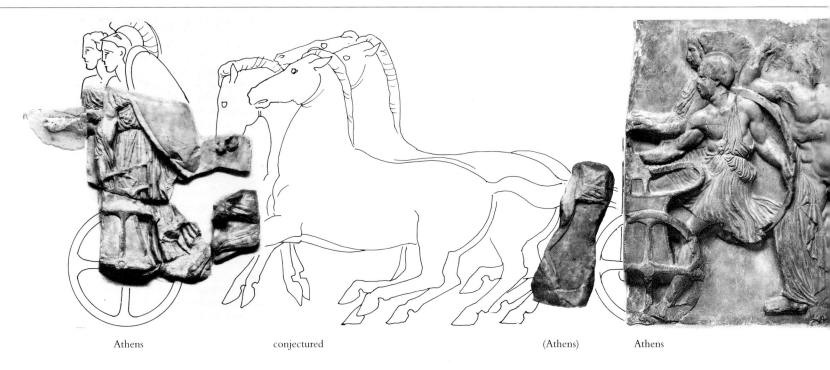

Athens   conjectured   (Athens)   Athens

The North Frieze

London   conjectured

A marshal (N65) leaps out of the way so as not to be run down by the chariot behind. His posture, naked body lurching forward and head turned back, is reminiscent of that of the marshal at the head of the chariot parade (N44). Such repeated figures add cohesion and continuity to the composition, and the moving-forward, glancing-backward attitude is found again and again. The carving of block XXIII is especially accomplished, with a pleasing contrast between the fluid 'river' of drapery falling down the chest of the soldier (N64) and the taut musculature of the solid form beneath. Then

again we may notice the studied interplay between the trailing arm of the soldier, opening to reveal the underside of the shield, and the trailing leg of the marshal, whose cloak opens to expose the body beneath.

It is difficult to say whether the foot soldier N64 is letting himself down from the chariot, as it slows, or hauling himself up, as it moves off. This ambivalence is perhaps deliberate, providing a pivotal point on which the action turns from vehicles drawing near their goal to those pulling away from a starting post.

(Athens)   London   (later window)   (Athens)   London and Athens   London

The North Frieze

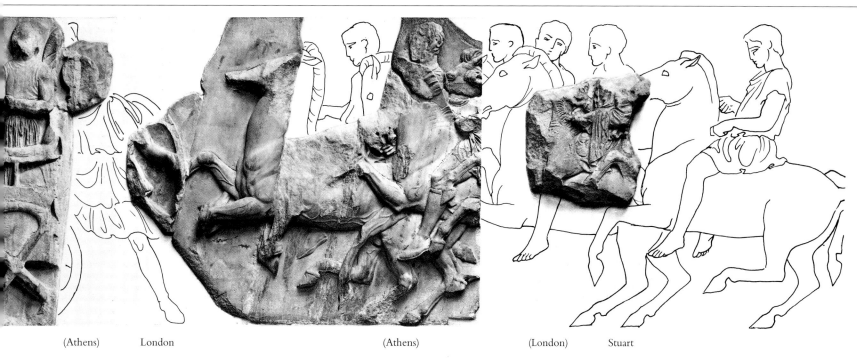

(Athens)   London   (Athens)   (London)   Stuart

The hindmost chariot in the sequence is stationary. A groom (N72) holds the halter, while the charioteer takes up the reins in readiness for the 'off'. A foot soldier (N74) grasps the guard rail of the carriage and hauls himself up. He looks back, and this, together with the trailing arm and shield, serves to link the chariot parade with the cavalcade that follows. The tails of the horses are arched in anticipation of the race ahead, but the overall scheme of block XXVIII seems awkward and curiously static in comparison with what we see elsewhere on the frieze. The charioteer, in particular, exhibits an archaic frontality which jars with the easy naturalism of the Phidian style.

The leading horseman (N75) of the northern cavalcade reins in his mount, so as not to seem to run into the back of the stationary chariot. The change in subject matter is further anticipated in the grouping of the horsemen behind, who are closely bunched with the action of slowing down and checking pace.

London   conjectured   (Athens)   London

The North Frieze

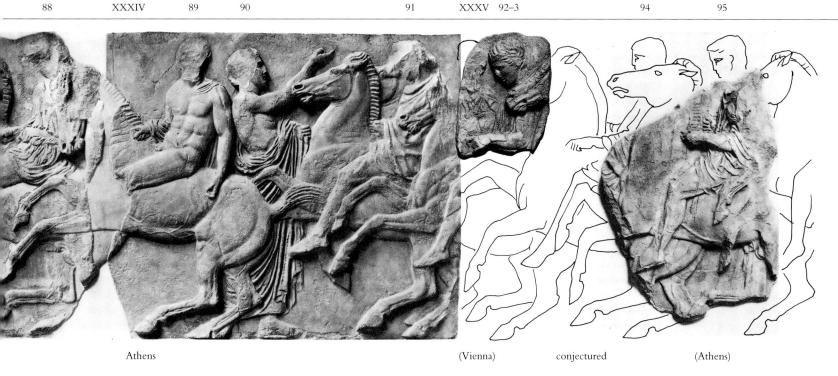

Athens   (Vienna)   conjectured   (Athens)

Marshals appear frequently in the chariot race but not in the horse parade. Here a solitary official (N90) beckons to the oncoming riders. Close by, a horseman (N89) looks back to check on the progress of his companions.

Such figures looking back over the shoulder serve at irregular intervals to mark the passage of the ride-past. Almost invariably they occupy the plane nearest to the viewer.

Athens

London

London

The North Frieze

London   London   London

The horsemen of the north frieze are composed of a series of phalanxes overlapping one on another. As in the south frieze, the total number of horsemen is sixty, but here the divisions are not regular. A tentative reconstruction of the plan of the north cavalcade consists of ten ranks of horsemen, each rank marked by a horse placed at the front. The position of each front horse is shown on the diagram below.

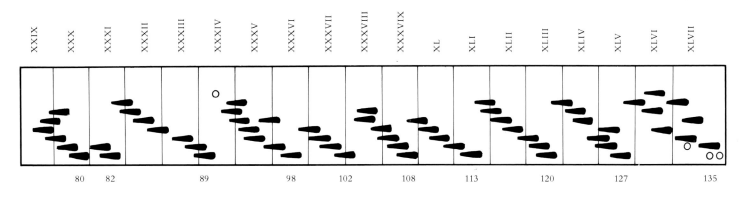

(Athens)   London   London

The horsemen of the north frieze are much less regular in their grouping
than those of the south. Here we do not find the same division of riders
into ten ranks of six identically dressed figures, overlapping one on another.
Instead, there is a great deal more variation, both in dress and in composition.
Some are heavily draped in mantle and tunic, while others are all but naked.
Some ride bareheaded, while others wear a distinctive form of cap which
seems to have been adopted from the native dress of the ancient Thracians,
whose homeland lay to the north of Greece. In the instance of figure N118,
body armour is worn with a crested helmet. On figure N119 we see the

The North Frieze

ear-flaps and neck-piece hanging down, while on figure N122 these are caught by the wind and whipped back.

Dress is used as one means of distinguishing the individual riders, while another is the position at which the head is held. Given the height of the frieze from the ground, it would not have been appropriate to attempt a rendering of individualised facial features. Such subtleties would be lost on the spectator at such a distance. In any case, the convention of Greek art at this period required the human face to be portrayed as a generalised type. Here, accordingly, the persona of the horsemen is that of ideal youth, with the same carefully measured features and sober, almost sullen expression. It would not be true, however, to say that each head is identical to the next. Apart from the device of different headgear, there is the clever suggestion of mood by varying the angle at which the head is held. Thus some riders possess an air of confidence with a level gaze directed straight ahead; others seem reflective, even melancholy, as they dip their chins and look down; while in a third group there are those who seem anxious as they direct their glance back over their shoulder.

(Athens)   London   (Athens)   London

The cavalcade of the north frieze, like the chariot sequence ahead, begins with stationary figures. A boy (N136) is caught in the action of tying a girdle around the waist of the waiting horseman (N135). The heads of the youth and of the boy are both dipped and this, together with their relaxed *contrapposto*, lends an air of quiet to the scene. The head of the standing horse is also tucked in as if in answer to that of its master. The figure (N133) ahead of this pair provides a stark contrast with the first. He too stands by his horse, but this creature seems eager to be off as it rears in anticipation. He restrains it with his right arm, while the left is raised to the head with the index finger extended. This gesture was intended as a signal and will be seen again shortly. His head is turned back and his lithe, all but naked body seems taut with the frustration of waiting for an unprepared friend. This dramatic figure leads us briskly into the cavalcade proper, which begins with the mounted figure N131. He wears a *chlamys* and a broad-brimmed sun hat thrown back on the shoulder. He checks the pace of his prancing horse and looks round to observe the situation at the rear, seemingly anxious not to leave his unmounted companions behind.

The West Frieze

London   London

The West Frieze

Athens

At the corner of the west frieze a marshal stands with head turned back towards the advancing riders. Both appear to be reining in their mounts, and the leading horseman turns round to look back. As he does so he raises his left hand to his head in a gesture very similar to that of N133. There are a number of points of comparison between these two figures. One is mounted and the other standing, but both look back, both signal with the left arm raised and both wear a cloak that is pulled close against the neck, while billowing out to the side. This similarity is not coincidental: with w2 the cavalcade must break to allow the waiting marshal to lead the eye around the corner, while N133 serves to conclude the momentary interlude occasioned by the dressing incident of N135. Figures w2 and N133 respectively open and close the passage of the cavalcade around the north-west corner.

The marshal w1 provides a strong vertical accent, echoed in the staff he once held in his right hand, at a point where the cavalcade may seem in danger of riding off the edge. The horses of w2 and 3 are reined in, as if in answer to his intimidating stare. He blocks their passage but he has a double purpose, both to guard the corner and to introduce the spectator to what lies around it. He looks in one direction, but the arch of his right side and the turn of his right foot seem to invite the eye to follow around the corner of the frieze and onto the north side.

Athens   Athens

The West Frieze

as   Athens

The cavalcade of the west frieze is not continuous, and although there are pairs of mounted riders putting the horses through their paces, these are interspersed with figures who represent scenes of preparation. Figure w12, for example, has one foot raised on a mounting block in order to adjust his footwear. Two riders approach him, while behind them w15 has difficulty in preventing his mount from joining them. This magnificent creature, full of fiery spirit, is one of the most remarkable horses of the frieze and is also commanded by an unusual figure. The head is now lost from the actual stone, but it was preserved in Elgin's day and from his cast we see it bearded and wearing a close-fitting cap with a long tail. His tunic is fixed on one shoulder only, and below the raised left arm his cloak is a flurry of folds. The apparent majesty of this horse and rider has given rise to the fancy that together they are an allegory of Pericles attempting to control the Athenian Democracy. This no longer seems probable, but the beard may indicate the status of a commander within the cavalry.

Athens   Athens

The West Frieze

ens

Athens

An unusual feature of the west frieze is that, whereas on the north, south and east sides there is considerable overlapping of figures from one slab to the next, here each rider or group of figures is contained within the frame of the block. A hoof or tail may be carried over, but the amount of overlapping is minimal. This observation raises the question of how the frieze was carved; whether, as some believe, it was executed on the ground and subsequently lifted into place, or whether it was carved *in situ*. Here, at least, where there is little overlapping, it is conceivable that the individual blocks were carved separately at ground level, but it seems more likely that the entire frieze was carved on the building.

Athens   Athens   (London)

The West Frieze

                Athens

The general sense of direction of the west frieze is from right to left, and the subject is usually taken as being preparatory to the cavalcade of the north frieze. Towards the south-west angle, however, some acknowledgment is made of the southern cavalcade and a number of figures, including one horse, turn in that direction. The motif of one foot raised on a mounting block, already seen in w12, is repeated in w29 and, although his mount faces north, this figure looks to the south. At the corner itself a figure, ostensibly arranging his mantle, is carefully designed to introduce the south frieze with arms raised and a strong *contrapposto* inclining to the right.

PLATE I

PLATE II

PLATE III

PLATE IV

PLATE V

PLATE VI

Illustration Acknowledgements

Figs 10, 11, 12, 14, 18 and 20 are drawn by Sue Bird. Fig. 1 is after G. Niemann; Fig. 2 after W. H. Plommer, 'Three Attic temples', *Annual of the British School at Athens* 45 (1950), pl. 7; Fig. 5 from F. Fanelli, *Atene Attica* (Venice 1707); Fig. 6 after A. K. Orlandos; Fig. 7 from G. P. Stevens, 'The Periclean entrance court of the Acropolis of Athens', *Hesperia* 5, no. 4 (1936), frontis; Fig. 8 after J. Travlos; Fig. 16 from R. Stillwell, 'The Panathenaic frieze', *Hesperia* 38 (1969), pl. 63.14; Fig. 19 (Acropolis Museum 396) from B. Graef and E. Langlotz, *Die Antiken Vasen von der Akropolis zu Athen* (Berlin 1933), vol. 2, pl. 22; Fig. 21 (Berlin 2537) from *Monumenti Inediti* 10 (Rome 1877), pl. 39. Fig. 4: Royal Ontario Museum, Toronto. Fig. 15: O. Palagia. Fig. 17: Metropolitan Museum of Art, New York (27.45). Plates I, III and IV: I. Jenkins. Plate II: Birmingham City Museum and Art Gallery. All other photos British Museum.

Index